TWO GREAT TRUTHS

TWO GREAT TRUTHS

A NEW SYNTHESIS OF SCIENTIFIC NATURALISM AND CHRISTIAN FAITH

David Ray Griffin

Westminster John Knox Press
LOUISVILLE • LONDON

Scripture quotations from the New Revised Standard Version of the Bible are copyright © 1989 by the Division of Christian Education of the National Council of the Churches of Christ in the U.S.A. and are used by permission.

Book design by Sharon Adams
Cover design by Eric Walljasper, Minneapolis, MN

First edition
Published by Westminster John Knox Press
Louisville, Kentucky

This book is printed on acid-free paper that meets the American National Standards Institute Z39.48 standard. ∞

PRINTED IN THE UNITED STATES OF AMERICA

05 06 07 08 09 10 11 12 13—10 9 8 7 6 5 4 3 2

Library of Congress Cataloging-in-Publication Data

Griffin, David Ray, 1939–
    Two great truths : a new synthesis of scientific naturalism and Christian faith / David Ray Griffin.
        p. cm.
    Includes bibliographical references and index.
    ISBN-13: 978-0-664-22773-9 (alk. paper)
    ISBN-10: 0-664-22773-2 (alk. paper)
    1. Religion and science. 2. Naturalism—Religious aspects—Christianity.
I. Title.

BL240.3.G75 2004
261.5'5—dc22

2004043024

Contents

Foreword

Howard J. Van Till

About three years ago I had occasion to be in correspondence with David Ray Griffin, whom I had not yet met personally. In passing, he mentioned that he had critically engaged some of my work in his book *Religion and Scientific Naturalism* (Albany: SUNY Press, 2000) and suggested that I might find his comments "interesting."

At the time I felt no particular sense of urgency to see what criticism he might have offered. My work on the interaction between Christian belief and the natural sciences had already received what I judged to be more than its fair share of critical commentary over the years, including four years of questioning by an investigative committee of the Calvin College Board of Trustees. Most of the criticism of my work came from the conservative end of the theological spectrum—from the broad evangelical Christian community and from the Reformed theological tradition into which I had been born. I must also admit that I found the majority of this critical commentary to be rather predictable and that it rarely stimulated me to explore new lines of thought.

Thoroughly trained in a Calvinist community that treasured its carefully crafted and comprehensive view of life and the world, I knew that we Christians were up against a tough enemy out there in the larger world, especially in the secular academy. Our chief adversary in the battle among worldviews was an atheistic system of thought that now permeated Western culture—a worldview rooted in the spiritual decline triggered by the Enlightenment and nourished by the advance of the scientific enterprise. Its name was "naturalism."

All naturalism, as I was initially conditioned to think of it, denied the reality of God and put nature in God's place. This naturalism was built on the false premise that nature is, in Carl Sagan's oft-quoted opening line of his PBS series *Cosmos,* "all that is or ever was or ever will be." Naturalism was, without a hint of doubt in the minds of my mentors, the enemy of theism. It had no place for the supernatural, no place for the sort of divine action so often highlighted in the telling of the Judeo-Christian story—God parting the Red Sea and making axe heads float; Jesus turning water into wine and multiplying a few loaves and fish into food for thousands—signs, wonders, and all manner of supernatural miracles that demonstrated divine power and authority.

But the association of naturalism with the sciences puzzled me. In the course of earning degrees in physics and doing observational research in astronomy I had gained a high respect for both the professional competence and the intellectual integrity that I observed in scientific practice. How could the science I loved be associated with a worldview so loathed? Were the natural sciences really providing ammunition for the enemy of Christianity?

There were a number of readily available ways to get around the appearance of conflict between a naturalistic science and my traditional Calvinism. One was to rest in the comfort that the naturalism actually employed by the sciences was merely *methodological* (about how science was practiced) and not *ontological* (about the ultimate nature of what exists). As a method of investigating the properties and behavior of the physical universe, natural science is limited in its competence to deal only with things physical—things such as quarks and quasars, atoms and molecules, stars and planets, bacteria and buffalo. Questions regarding divine action are, therefore, beyond the scope of its investigative capabilities. *Methodological naturalism* is a statement about the character of natural science, not about the character of reality. As such, it can say nothing about the being or nonbeing of God. Traditional theism, then, is safe from defeat by a scientific enterprise that can say nothing about the power and authority of divine action.

But, alas, the most vocal Christian critics of science were seldom persuaded by this appeal to methodological naturalism. After all, it was commonly argued (or at least implied) that the ultimate source of *methodological* naturalism was really *ontological* naturalism (what Griffin calls either "maximal naturalism" or "materialism")—the worldview that denies both the being and the supernatural power of God. Through the eyes of its critics, methodological naturalism was seen as little more than a camouflaged version of materialism. Some critics made the rhetorically tendentious choice to refer to it by the more explicitly pejorative label "provisional atheism." Its real agenda, some suspected, was to allow the wolf of materialism to sneak into the public educational system, mischievously dressed in the sheep's clothing of a harmless methodological principle. Naturalism's critics were, of course, far too smart to be fooled by so simple a disguise. The malodorous presence of the wolf was still detectable, and a wolf disguised could be considered even more dangerous and repugnant than one who dared to come in plain view.

In the face of this sort of rhetoric, I generally chose not to use the term "methodological naturalism." The suggestion of guilt by association can be an effective rhetorical strategy, especially when directed toward audiences that are not accustomed to making fine distinctions. But I did not really find the setting aside of this term to be a particularly serious loss. My concern had not been to protect science from criticism but to find ways of talking fruitfully about the universe as known by the natural sciences and about God's action within it. In the context of North America's obsession with the creation/evolution debate, the character of the universe's formational history and the role of divine action in the actualization of new creatures have become especially important issues. But that debate has, in my judgment, degenerated into a futile shouting match. Among my major complaints about the debate as it is most commonly conducted is the fact that the "creation" side is so often associated with an anti-science biblical literalism, and the "evolution" side so often associated with a God-denying materialism. I wanted no part of either of these two extreme positions.

The relatively conservative Christian audience to which I most frequently addressed my critique of the creation/evolution discussion was often very skeptical of modern science, especially of its theories regarding the evolutionary development of the universe and of "all creatures great and small" within it. The roots of this skepticism were clumped primarily in two areas: (1) a concern that faithfulness to the Scriptures required the employment of some form of supernaturalism in portraying divine creative action; and (2) an association of the natural sciences, especially their theories of evolutionary development, with a form of scientific naturalism that was presumed to be forever irreconcilable with the Christian faith.

Given that circumstance, and given my grounding in the Calvinist view of life and the world, my strategy for encouraging a more constructive and mutually informative relationship between Christian theology and natural science was directed toward the task of correcting what I judged to be misunderstandings in each of those two areas.

Regarding the requirements of the Bible. While maintaining a high regard for the theological relevance of the Scriptures, I argued that the various biblical portraits of divine creative action ought not to be read as if they were chronicles of particular divine acts. Genesis 1, for instance, ought not to be read as a what-happened-and-when account depicting episodes of supernatural form-imposing action. Although I did not categorically rule out the *possibility* of supernatural (coercive) action, I did candidly express my judgment that form-conferring supernatural interventions were *unnecessary* for the actualization of new creaturely forms in the course of time.

Regarding the association of the sciences with an antitheistic naturalism. I took this association to be misguided. Given the limited competence of the sciences to deal only with natural phenomena, I argued that the more fundamental and important questions—questions of interest to theology and metaphysics, for example—remained open for unbiased examination. Naturalism (the several differing forms of which I did not adequately distinguish at that time) had no right to claim ownership of the sciences, and the sciences had no means to discredit sound theology. That being the case, any association of the natural sciences with a God-denying naturalism was, I argued, simply unwarranted.

For a combination of scientific and theological reasons I crafted an approach that avoided both extremes of the usual creation-evolution shouting match. From the theological/biblical side I saw no reason to insist on any form of *episodic creationist* strategy that posited occasional episodes of form-conferring supernatural intervention as the only means by which certain organisms or biotic systems could be actualized.*

From the scientific side I saw no reason to doubt that continuing empirical work would eventually lead to the discovery of all the formational resources, potentialities, and capabilities that would have been needed to actualize not only inanimate physical structures, from atoms to galaxies, but also the whole array of biological systems that are participants in the universe's formational history. Given those judgments, it seemed entirely unnecessary for theology to portray God's creative action in interventionist terms or for science to change its manner of investigating the universe's formational history.

At the same time, however, and still content to operate within the spirit of my Calvinist heritage, I saw no reason to rule out the possibility of supernatural divine action. In fact, it was clear to me that if I wished to maintain any influence at all within the Reformed and evangelical Christian communities, it was strategically essential that I be very explicit in stating my openness to the possibility of supernatural action. My usual way of stating this position was this: Although I judged that supernatural interventions were wholly unnecessary for the actualization of new structures and life forms in the course of the universe's formational history, I did not categorically rule out the possibility for God to act supernaturally. God is, of course, free to act in any way that is consistent with God's being and God's will. My positing that supernatural intervention was unnecessary for the formation of new creatures did not change that state of affairs. I eventually called this approach the "fully gifted Creation" perspective: The Creation to which God gave

---

*What I here call "episodic creationism" is essentially the same as what has more commonly been called "special creationism." The term *special* creationism arose nearly two centuries ago in the context of envisioning God to have formed each individual *species* (or some broader classification category) of living things. I now choose to use the term *episodic* creationism to call attention to the contemporary emphasis on the idea that God formed at least some life forms, or parts of life forms, by means of a succession of *episodes* of form-conferring supernatural intervention.

being (*ex nihilo*, I presumed) was fully gifted by God from the out-set with all of the requisite formational resources, potentialities, and capabilities to make its evolutionary development possible, without need of any episodes of form-conferring supernatural interven-tion.* In retrospect, it seems that I was content to do without the concept of supernatural intervention, especially as the means for actualizing new creaturely forms, but was not yet prepared to rule out the possibility of supernatural action categorically.

As I saw it, the fully gifted Creation approach gave due credit both to God's creativity (in conceptualizing a Creation that could accom-plish something so remarkable) and to God's generosity (in giving such richness of being to the Creation). It was also an approach that gave due respect to the sciences for all that they had learned about the formational history of the universe and the processes that had con-tributed to it.

Not surprisingly, reactions to this approach have varied widely. Conservative Christians prone to biblical literalism have found it dif-ficult to accommodate any approach that accepts the fourteen-billion-year chronology generated by the historical natural sciences. Furthermore, in North American culture the word "evolution" has become so closely associated with materialism that any approach that accepts the scientific concept of evolutionary development, as my approach did, is perceived among many conservative Christians as having the equivalent of 2.999 strikes against it. This combination of biblical literalism and antievolution sentiment makes acceptance of the fully gifted Creation perspective very problematic, if not impos-sible, among fundamentalist Christians.

But there is a significant fraction of traditional supernatural theists who are not committed either to biblical literalism or to the rejection of evolutionary theory. Many members of the Calvinist community

---

*My development of this approach can be found in several publications. See, for example, "The Fully Gifted Creation," published as a chapter in *Three Views on Creation and Evolution*, edited by J. P. Moreland and John Mark Reynolds (Grand Rapids: Zondervan, 1999), 161–247; "Science and Christian Theology as Partners in Theorizing," published as a chapter in *Science and Christianity: Four Views*, edited by Richard F. Carlson (Downers Grove, Ill.: InterVarsity Press, 2000), 196–236; "The Creation: Intelligently Designed or Optimally Equipped?" *Theology Today* 55, no. 3 (October 1998): 344–64; and "Is the Creation a *Right Stuff* Universe?" *Perspectives on Science and Christian Faith* 54, no. 4 (December 2002): 232–39.

fall into this category, as do numerous members of the broader evangelical Christian community.*

For many of these people, the fully gifted Creation perspective (sometimes called the *evolving Creation* perspective) functions fruitfully as a means of placing Christian belief and scientific investigation into a nonadversarial and mutually informative relationship.

Some, however, remain skeptical. One response that I frequently encounter is that "it sounds too much like deism." Where is there any explicit reference to divine action in the process of actualizing novel structures? Can we not point to any instances of empirical evidence that God has been active in the actualizing of new forms of life? Does God do nothing to form new creatures? Has God become an inactive and unnecessary adornment to standard scientific theorizing about evolution?

These are noteworthy concerns that deserve thoughtful attention. Let me now state them in another way by introducing a new term. In developing my viewpoint I have found it helpful to define the "formational economy" of the universe to be the set of all of the universe's resources, potentialities and formational capabilities that have ever contributed to the actualization of new physical structures and new life forms in the course of its formational history.†

In the context of discussions regarding the role of divine action in this history, the following particularly fundamental question inevitably arises: Is the universe's formational economy sufficiently robust (amply equipped) to make possible the actualization of every type of physical structure and life form that has ever existed without need for occasional form-conferring divine interventions? To answer "yes" to this question is to affirm what I call the Robust Formational Economy Principle (RFEP).

---

*For several representatives of this category, see Keith Miller, ed., *Perspectives on an Evolving Creation* (Grand Rapids: Wm. B. Eerdmans Publishing Co., 2003), which includes a chapter titled "Is the Universe Capable of Evolving?" in which I present the fully gifted Creation approach as one that evangelical Christians could find acceptable.

†In this definition, "resources" refers to such things as elementary particles, their modes of interaction, and the space-time context in which they interact; "capabilities" refers to what things can do, such as the capabilities of atoms to organize into molecules; and "potentialities" refers primarily to structures that would, if once assembled, be sustainable or functional. In a sense, the "formational economy" of the universe is the sum of what the universe *is*, how it can *change*, and what it is able to *become*.

This RFEP includes such concepts as the "fine-tuning" of the universe—the values of the fundamental physical parameters are just right to make possible the development of carbon-based life somewhere in the universe—but its concerns are at once more basic and more comprehensive. To speak of a universe whose basic parameter values are fine-tuned for life already assumes the existence and character of things such as elementary particles, atoms, planets, stars, and galaxies in an expanding spatial framework. The fine-tuning feature applies to the particular values of the physical constants associated with this set of entities. The RFEP does not take such entities for granted, and calls attention to the fact that the very existence and nature of these various components are by no means self-explanatory, and that they must be recognized as unexplained features of our universe. That there should exist the specific array of elementary particles that we observe is not self-evident. That they should interact in the particular manner they do is not self-evident. That they should possess the formational capabilities to actualize functional structures such as stars or starfish is not self-evident. It is remarkable enough that there exists *something* rather than *nothing*. Even more remarkable, I suggest, is that the something that exists is a universe characterized by a robust formational economy—a universe that has all the "right stuff" to self-organize into atoms, molecules, planets, stars, galaxies, and myriad forms of life.

Nevertheless, the natural sciences today do presume the universe to satisfy the RFEP. This principle is a seldom stated but profoundly fundamental presupposition of the historical natural sciences. Christian critics of these sciences could, of course, argue that the RFEP cannot be proved and that it could conceivably be false. At the same time, however, it must be said that presuming the universe to satisfy the RFEP has been the foundation for the astounding fruitfulness of the historical natural sciences. Fruitfulness of this degree goes a long way toward building warranted confidence in any principle or physical law. As for the laws of thermodynamics, so also for the Robust Formational Economy Principle.

But scientific fruitfulness is not the only reason for accepting the RFEP. The fully gifted Creation perspective, as outlined above, also presumes that the universe satisfies the RFEP—as a manifestation of the Creator's creativity and generosity. I might even be inclined to include it in a contemporary version of Psalm 104. But, and here's the rub, the RFEP is also presumed true by proponents of maximal (atheistic) naturalism. Given its exclusion of any form of deity, materialism has little choice but to take the universe's robust formational economy as an unexplained given. If the fully gifted Creation perspective makes the same assumption as does maximal naturalism regarding the applicability of the RFEP, then has all reference to divine action in the formational history of the universe been made unnecessary, superficial at best? If there are no gaps (missing elements) in the universe's formational economy, is divine action categorically ruled out? In effect, this is the same question I asked a moment ago: Does God do nothing to form new creatures?

A number of responses can be offered here: (1) Traditional supernatural theism (including the Calvinist heritage in which I was brought up), building on the concept of *creatio ex nihilo*, maintains that God's continuing action of *sustaining* the Creation is just as essential as God's action of giving it being in the first place. The RFEP does posit something important about the nature of this created universe but, by itself, does not at all negate either the possibility or the necessity of God's sustaining action. (2) Orthodox Christian theology has never, to my knowledge, posited that supernatural divine action was possible only within gaps (opened up by missing elements) in the Creation's formational economy. That being the case, the absence of such gaps is no theological loss whatsoever.

After offering these and other considerations in defense of the proposition that there is no compelling reason for supernatural theists to reject the fully gifted Creation perspective or the Robust Formational Economy Principle that it entails, I have found that the most common response remains, "It still sounds too much like deism to me." I find this response telling. In effect, the message it conveys to me is this: Remove the *need* for occasional divine acts of form-conferring supernatural intervention, and the majority of Christians today become extremely uncomfortable. Supernaturalism is deeply embedded in contemporary Christianity, and any attempt to make even one portion (specifically the episodic creationist portion) of that action unnecessary will be met with intense resistance, or at least deep skepticism. I believe it is the case that the majority of Christians today cannot imagine a Christian belief system that excludes supernaturalism.

As noted earlier, I long stood in a narrow space adjacent to this majority view. I found supernatural intervention unnecessary as a means of forming novel creatures, but I was not yet prepared to exclude supernaturalism categorically. This is where I found David Griffin's critical engagement of my perspective especially helpful. When, after a brief delay, I bought a copy of Griffin's *Religion and Scientific Naturalism* and read his criticism of my approach, I found something far more helpful than I had been willing to anticipate.* In fact, as I have told many audiences in the last couple of years, I found his criticism to be the most helpful that I had ever received. To summarize it as succinctly as I can, these are the two principal challenges that he offered for my consideration:

Dare to be consistent in regard to supernatural divine action. If, as I had already maintained, supernatural action is unnecessary for something as astounding as the formational history of the entire universe, then why hold to the need, or even the possibility, for occasional episodes of coercive supernatural action in any other arena? Griffin's carefully crafted development of a concept of variable and effective, but noncoercive, divine action struck me as an attractive alternative to the traditional concept of supernatural divine action held by the majority of Christians today. Not only does it offer a way to appreciate the ubiquity of noncoercive divine action in the natural world, it also offers a way to avoid some of the dreadful problems of theodicy that inevitably accompany traditional supernaturalism and its doctrine of divine omnipotence.

Naturalism and theism need not be enemies: Naturalism comes in significantly different forms that must be carefully distinguished from one another. *Maximal naturalism* (or materialism) does indeed preclude the existence of God, and it builds its worldview on the premise that nature is all there is. Other forms of naturalism, however, require no denial of God and no categorical rejection of divine action.

* I highly recommend Griffin's *Religion and Scientific Naturalism*, and his *Reenchantment without Supernaturalism.*

Minimal naturalism (or scientific naturalism stripped of any association with materialism), for example, rejects only supernatural (coercive) action and remains agnostic with regard to noncoercive divine action. Griffin's recommendation to spokespersons for science is to rid the sciences of their recently acquired association with maximal naturalism and to recognize that minimal naturalism is not only sufficient for the work of the natural sciences but also provides a superior metaphysical foundation for the scientific enterprise. *Naturalistic theism*—yet another form of naturalism—joins minimal (scientific) naturalism in rejecting supernaturalism but then proceeds to develop an enriched concept of natural phenomena by incorporating effective but noncoercive divine action as an essential component of all natural processes.

Griffin's two challenges to my earlier strategy have been essential to my continuing spiritual and theological odyssey. Learning to rearticulate my experience of the sacred without the familiar category of supernatural action and learning to appreciate the ability of naturalistic theism to provide me with an effective conceptual vocabulary for reflecting on the experience of God's active presence in everyday phenomena has been a remarkably rewarding exercise. At the beginning of this essay I confessed that I found most earlier criticism of my work rather predictable and that it failed to stimulate much new thinking. David Ray Griffin's criticism, on the other hand, awakened me to new and fruitful approaches for making theological sense out of the human experience, including the experience of scientific investigation and theorizing.

That is why I recommended Griffin's work to my pastor, Richard A. Rhem, at Christ Community Church in Spring Lake, Michigan. And that is why I encouraged our Center for Religion and Life to invite Dr. Griffin to present a series of lectures on these issues in October 2002. What follows are the written versions of those lectures. I am delighted to see them in print. For anyone who is looking for a way to understand how natural science and Christian belief came to be so alienated from one another, here is a succinct analysis of the history of that process of alienation. Here also is the way to reverse it, to rid scientific naturalism of the materialistic baggage that it has accumulated and rid Christian theology of the supernaturalism that has come to dominate its modern expression. Restored versions of both scientific naturalism and Christian theology can be the best of friends, each encouraging the other to develop its God-given gifts. Sounds like a good marriage, doesn't it?

Preface

*T*he modern world has presented the Christian faith with many deep challenges, both practical and intellectual. The present book focuses on one of the intellectual challenges to Christian faith—the widespread view that it is in conflict with the worldview of modern science. This question is often posed in terms of the relation between "science and religion," "science and Christian faith," or "science and theology." But this phrasing—by suggesting that Christian faith might be in conflict with science itself—reflects an earlier era, when Christian faith was still wedded to ideas such as that the earth is the center of the universe, that it is only a few thousand years old, or that human beings were created directly and not through a long evolutionary process, ideas that were challenged by discoveries made by the empirical sciences, such as astronomy, geology, and biology.

To be sure, conservative to fundamentalist forms of Christian faith that are wedded to such ideas still exist, so in those circles the question of the relation of faith to science can still be a burning one. But the more serious challenge today comes not from science itself but from the worldview with which it is associated, which is widely called *scientific naturalism*. This challenge is more serious because it confronts not only conservative to fundamentalist Christians but all Christians, including modern liberal Christians who fully accept the authority of science to decide matters of empirical fact. This challenge exists because scientific naturalism has been widely understood as a worldview that rules out not only conservative to fundamentalist forms of Christian faith but any significantly religious worldview whatsoever.

Part of the solution to this problem involves the realization that a deep confusion has run through the discussion of whether scientific naturalism is compatible with Christian faith. This confusion involves two meanings of scientific naturalism. In the generic or minimal sense, scientific naturalism is simply the denial of supernatural interruptions of the world's basic causal processes. Naturalism in this sense is not a new idea. It was developed by pre-Socratic Greek philosophers and was fully embodied in the philosophies of Plato and Aristotle. Scientific naturalism in this sense does, to be sure, conflict with many forms of Christian faith that have appeared through the centuries, but it is not obvious that it conflicts with Christian faith itself or even rules out a robust version of Christian faith. I argue that it does not. Indeed, I suggest that scientific naturalism in the generic sense is a great truth that should be enthusiastically adopted by Christians.

However, as this great truth was being recovered in the nineteenth century, it was embodied in an extremely restrictive version of naturalism, which I call scientific naturalism$_{sam}$ for reasons that will be explained. This version of scientific naturalism *is* incompatible with Christian faith and any other significantly religious perspective on the universe. A central task of Christian theology today, therefore, is the twofold task of distinguishing clearly between these two meanings of *scientific naturalism* and then, if possible, pointing to another version of naturalism that is compatible with Christian faith.

Overcoming the distorted form of scientific naturalism would, however, not by itself overcome the apparent conflict between Christian faith and scientific naturalism. This is the case because the dominant form of Christian faith in previous centuries, which is generally inherited by Christians today, is incompatible even with scientific naturalism in the minimal sense. In relation to this problem, I argue that just as scientific naturalism is a great truth that got distorted, so is Christian faith.

Here the central distortion involves a nonbiblical doctrine of "creation out of nothing," which was introduced near the end of the second Christian century. Besides producing a doctrine of divine omnipotence that led to an insoluble problem of evil, this postbiblical doctrine has been the primary basis for thinking that Christian faith is incompatible with scientific naturalism in the generic sense. The two can be seen to be fully compatible only when this distorted view of divine creation is overcome. This can be done, I suggest, by following Nicolas Berdyaev's proposal that we take the "nothing" in "creation out of nothing" to mean *relative*, rather than *absolute*, nothingness, thereby returning to the biblical view, according to which God created our world out of chaos ("a formless void"). This seemingly slight change has enormous implications for virtually every issue, from the problem of evil to Christology to religious pluralism.

I deeply believe that both scientific naturalism, understood in the generic sense, and Christian faith, understood to mean the primary doctrines of the Christian good news, are great truths. If this is the case, then, since truth is one, scientific naturalism and Christian faith must be mutually compatible. They have come into conflict because each tradition has distorted its own truth, turning it into a falsehood.

The fact that I see both truth and distortion on each side means that my treatment of the apparent conflict between science and Christian faith differs from most popular treatments, which tend to see mainly truth on one side and mainly error on the other. Many leading representatives of the scientific community, convinced that its worldview is close to the final truth about the universe, think that the beliefs of Christianity and other religions, insofar as they differ from the scientific worldview of today, contain nothing but myth, illusion, and error.*

Likewise, many conservative to fundamentalist theologians, convinced that the worldview of their community is close to the final truth about reality, are convinced that scientific naturalism is completely false and that the conflict between science and religion will be resolved if, and only if, the scientific community returns to a supernaturalistic framework.†

My perspective suggests that there has been about the same amount of error on both sides of the debate but that there is also a very great truth being defended by each side—which helps explain why the debate has been so intense and seemingly interminable. I do not believe, however, that the debate is unresolvable. By sorting out the truth from the error on both sides, we can develop a worldview that

*For examples of this view, see my *Religion and Scientific Naturalism*, chap. 3.

†For my critique of a sophisticated version of this view, see my discussion of Phillip Johnson and Alvin Plantinga in chap. 3 of *Religion and Scientific Naturalism*.

can be held in common. This does not mean that science and Christian theology would become identical. They are and will remain very different enterprises, focusing on different aspects of the total truth. But they could share certain beliefs in common, in terms of which each community could recognize the validity of what the other is doing and in terms of which some people could participate fully in both communities, without holding one worldview on Sunday and another on working days.*

This book is based upon a series of lectures given October 4–6, 2002, at the invitation of the Center for Religion and Life at Christ Community Church in Spring Lake, Michigan. I am deeply grateful to this remarkable center, this remarkable congregation, and its remarkable pastor, Richard Rhem, for the opportunity to lay out my views on this topic. I am also grateful to Howard Van Till, at whose suggestion the invitation was offered, who also made several valuable suggestions for improvement while I was turning the lectures into this little book, and who graciously agreed to write the foreword. I wish also to express publicly my thanks to Howard and his wife, Betty, for their gracious hospitality.

As always, I thank my wife, Ann Jaqua, for her support. I hope that I have hereby produced a book that our grandsons—Dakota, Dylan, Matthew, Michael, Nicolas, and Van—might find helpful one of these days.

I am, finally, grateful to Jack Keller of Westminster John Knox Press for his enthusiasm for this book and for making the publication process as easy as possible.

*My position is a version of what Ian Barbour calls the "integrationist" approach. For his typology, along with illustrations of each type, see his *Religion in an Age of Science* and, for a briefer discussion, *When Science Meets Religion*.

Chapter 1

Scientific Naturalism

A Great Truth That Got Distorted

*C*hristian theologian John Cobb has suggested that every great tradition, such as Christianity or Buddhism, has a universal truth that members of other traditions should appropriate for themselves. Recognizing that modern science is also one of the great traditions, Cobb has encouraged fellows Christians not to resist "appropriation of the universal truth offered by modern science."[1] What is this universal truth that should be appropriated? It is, I suggest, the doctrine that has come to be called "scientific naturalism."

1. Scientific Naturalism

Many Christian thinkers, far from thinking of scientific naturalism as a great truth, have considered it a great falsehood. Rather than something to be appropriated, scientific naturalism is something to be slain—or at least something to be avoided, along with clichés, like the plague. Given the way scientific naturalism is usually understood—as a materialistic, atheistic worldview—I agree. It is incompatible with Christian faith and, in fact, with any significantly religious view of reality, and it is a false doctrine, whose falsity needs to be exposed.[2] But this materialistic, atheistic form of naturalism, insofar as it is presented as "the scientific worldview," is precisely what I mean by scientific naturalism in its distorted form.

In referring to scientific naturalism as a great truth, I am referring to what can be called naturalism in the *minimal* or *generic* sense. This

1

is the doctrine that the universe involves an extremely complex web of cause-and-effect relations; that every event occurs within this web, having causal antecedents and causal consequences; and that every event exemplifies a common set of causal principles. The scientific mentality, said Alfred North Whitehead, "instinctively holds that all things great and small are conceivable as exemplifications of general principles which reign throughout the natural order," so that "every detailed occurrence can be correlated with its antecedents in a perfectly definite manner, exemplifying general principles."[3] Naturalism is the doctrine that this causal web, with its general causal principles, cannot be interrupted from time to time.

Naturalism in this minimal sense does not entail atheism. There are theistic versions of naturalism. Naturalism in this minimal sense rules out only *supernaturalism*, defined as the doctrine that there is a supernatural being who, existing outside the otherwise universal web of cause-effect relations, can violate it. To emphasize the point that when I endorse naturalism I have in mind only the exclusion of supernaturalism, I sometimes call naturalism in this generic or minimal sense "naturalism$_{ns}$," with the "ns" standing for "nonsupernaturalistic."

To make even clearer what I do and do not mean by naturalism, let me contrast this meaning with another meaning often given the term. Naturalism, it is often said, is the doctrine that "nature is all there is," with "nature" here understood to mean the totality of all finite things, processes, and events.* Using "nati" to stand for "nature is all there is," we can refer to this doctrine as "naturalism$_{nati}$." Naturalism$_{nati}$, by specifying that there is nothing other than the totality of finite things, does rule out theism. If someone who defined naturalism as naturalism$_{nati}$ asked me whether I am a naturalist or a supernaturalist, I would have to say that I am a supernaturalist. But I resist using this term for my position because the term "supernaturalism" inevitably suggests the idea that there is a divine being who is beyond nature in the sense of being able to interrupt its most fundamental causal processes. Supernaturalism in this sense, I will argue in subsequent

---

*Naturalists understand nature, says Phillip E. Johnson, "to be 'all there is'" (*Reason in the Balance*, 38 n). This understanding of naturalism is illustrated by Gilbert Harman, who defines it as "the sensible thesis that *all* facts are facts of nature" (*The Nature of Morality*, 17).

chapters, has led to a distortion of Christian faith that has created insuperable problems for the Christian community. One of those problems is the apparent conflict it creates between Christian faith and science, given the fact that the scientific community during the past three centuries has come to presuppose naturalism$_{ns}$ so completely that a rejection of it now is unthinkable.

Having explained what I mean by "scientific naturalism" in the generic sense, I will next discuss the process through which this great truth emerged in the scientific tradition, and also how, tragically, it emerged in a distorted form, so that this great truth became an enormous falsehood.

2. The Emergence of Scientific Naturalism

In discussing the emergence of scientific naturalism, I am limiting my discussion to developments in the West.* For this discussion, I have drawn primarily on David Lindberg's definitive work, *The Beginnings of Western Science: The European Scientific Tradition in Philosophical, Religious, and Institutional Context, 600 B.C. to A.D. 1450.* As the subtitle of Lindberg's book indicates, the scientific mentality first developed in the sixth century B.C. in Greece. As late as the eighth and seventh centuries B.C., Greek culture, as represented in the works of Homer and Hesiod, had still fully accepted the idea of supernatural incursions into the world, as did other cultures at the time. As Lindberg says, the world of Homer and Hesiod was "a capricious world, in which nothing could be safely predicted because of the boundless possibilities of divine intervention."[4] With such a worldview, a tradition of scientific investigation could not have developed. But in the sixth century B.C., there arose a type of philosophy that portrayed the world as a "cosmos," that is, as an *ordered* world. The philosophers who developed this approach, such as Thales, Heraclitus, Anaximander, and Anaximenes, initiated what we think of as the

---

*The question of the degree to which similar developments may have occurred elsewhere, especially in China, is beyond the scope of this discussion. On China, see Joseph Needham's multivolume work, *Science and Civilization in China.*

scientific mentality. We would, to be sure, find most of their explanations primitive, "but what is of critical importance," points out Lindberg, "is that they exclude the gods. The explanations are entirely naturalistic."[5] Within this tradition, Lindberg adds, "A distinction between the natural and the supernatural was emerging; and there was a wide agreement that causes . . . are to be sought only in the nature of things," not, for example, in the "personal whim or the arbitrary fancies of the gods."[6]

Some of the philosophers in this naturalistic tradition were materialists, such as Democritus, who taught near the end of the fifth century B.C. According to Democritus, the world consisted of nothing but tiny atoms moving randomly in an infinite void. Democritus argued that these atoms, through their accidental collisions and combinations, accounted for all the features of our world, including our conscious experience.

One could be a naturalist, however, without being a materialist. For example, Pythagoras, the father of mathematics, affirmed the ultimate reality of numbers. Then in the fourth century B.C., Plato, who was influenced by Socrates as well as by Pythagoras, stressed the reality of ethical as well as mathematical forms. Central to Plato's cosmology was a doctrine of the human soul according to which it had the capacity to know these eternal forms. This soul also had freedom, thereby moral responsibility, and the capacity to survive bodily death. Plato's cosmology even included divine realities, including a creator and a world soul. However, as Lindberg points out, "Plato's deities never interrupt the course of nature. . . . Thus Plato's reintroduction of divinity does not represent a return to the unpredictability of the Homeric world."[7] Indeed, Plato had decided, in opposition to the materialists, that the world's order could not be explained by saying that it is immanent in physical things. This order could be explained only by attributing it to psyche— to mind or soul. Many previous philosophers had thought that if the world is to be portrayed as an ordered cosmos, the gods must be banished. But Plato restored divinity *to account for* this order.[8]

In portraying this world as having been brought about by a divine creator, but one who never interrupts its causal processes, Plato offered the world a *naturalistic theism* and hence a *theistic naturalism*. A crucial element in this philosophical theology is the idea that our world was created out of chaos, not out of absolute nothingness. This view involves a distinction between *our* world, which was created at a particular time in the past, and *the* world, meaning simply a realm of finite beings, which has always existed. Prior to the creation of *our* world, *the* world existed in a state of chaos. The divine creator created *our* world by bringing an ordered cosmos out of this chaotic state. The reason this point is so important is that it suggests that there is power inherent in the world, so that the creator is not absolutely omnipotent in the sense of being able to bring about any desired state of affairs by simply willing it. Plato emphasized this point, saying that although the creator sought to bring about the "best possible" result, the recalcitrance of the material with which the creator worked explains why our world is imperfect.

With his doctrine of the eternal forms, the human soul, and the divine creator, Plato had a rich naturalism that could do justice to at least many of the features of our world, including its evil. However, although the virtues of his system led to his having great influence, not everyone accepted all of his ideas.

One of those with different ideas was Plato's most famous student, Aristotle. Although Aristotle's cosmology, like Plato's, had a supreme divinity, this deity, the "unmoved mover," was not a personal agent who created our world. In fact, according to Aristotle, our world was not created at all, but is eternal, because Aristotle made no distinction between our world and *the* world. And although Aristotle spoke of the human soul, this soul, being defined as the form of the body, was not a distinct actuality that could survive the body's demise. So, although Aristotle's version of naturalism was richer than that of Plato's materialistic predecessors, it was considerably more restrictive than Plato's own version.

3. The Modification of Greek Naturalism in the Middle Ages

It is not surprising, therefore, that when Christian thinkers began relating the biblical cosmology to Greek philosophy, they found Plato most congenial. Indeed, throughout most of Christianity's first two centuries, Christian thinkers evidently saw no essential contradiction between the biblical view of creation and Plato's, as many second-century Christian philosophers employed his account of creation out of chaos. This sense of essential compatibility does not mean, of course, that there were no tensions. Given the biblical tradition's account of divinely caused miracles, Christian philosophers in effect modified the naturalism of Greek philosophy, allowing for occasional supernatural interruptions of the normal cause-effect relations. For some time, this belief in miracles existed in uneasy tension with the acceptance of a view of creation that, in Plato's mind, excluded the possibility of interruptions of the natural fabric. However, near the end of the second century, for reasons to be explained in the next chapter, several Christian theologians began insisting on the idea that God had created the world *ex nihilo*, or out of nothing, with the "nothing" understood to mean an absolute absence of finite beings. This idea very quickly became considered the orthodox Christian view, with the consequence that the idea of miraculous interruptions of the natural order was provided with a rationale: If the causal principles embodied in our world do not lie in the very nature of things, as Plato thought, but were freely created by God, they can be freely interrupted.

This rejection of Greek naturalism meant that the relation between Christianity and the Greek heritage was ambivalent. On the one hand, Christianity, which appreciated and employed the Greek heritage, preserved and transmitted it. Christianity did this through its patronage of Hellenistic schools, through its preservation of manuscripts and learning in the monasteries, and then by its support of the early universities in the late Middle Ages.[9] This task of preservation and transmission was an essential task, without which the emergence of modern natural science—which is what natural philosophy came to be called—would have been impossible.

Christianity was, to be sure, not the only tradition that had a hand in this process. From the eighth through the twelfth centuries, during which the Christian West was for the most part intellectually moribund, the Greek heritage, especially as embodied in Aristotle, was kept alive and developed almost exclusively in the Islamic world. It was largely through stimulation from the Islamic world that the Christian West began, in the twelfth and thirteenth centuries, to wrestle again with Greek thought, with Aristotle's influence now eclipsing Plato's. However, although the story of the development of Western science must give ample credit to the Islamic tradition, that tradition lost its preeminence in the thirteenth and fourteenth centuries, in part because it had failed to give scientific thought an institutional home.

In the West, by contrast, the church gave great support, including remarkable freedom, to the universities that began emerging in the twelfth century, thereby providing natural philosophy with an institutional home.[10] Accordingly, much of the credit for the emergence of modern science would have to go to the Christian tradition for its institutional support, even if that had been its only contribution, which it was not.* That is all on the one hand.

On the other hand, Christianity, with its doctrine of supernatural miracles, supported by the doctrine of creation out of nothing, undermined the naturalism of the Greek tradition. There is nothing surprising about this. Christians saw their religion as based on God's final revelation, to which all other ideas must be subordinated. Insofar as Christian theologians employed Greek philosophy, they quite naturally viewed it as "the handmaiden of the faith," to be used when possible, to be modified when necessary. This modification supported a worldview that was similar to that of Homer with regard to its conflict with a scientific mentality. John Hedley Brooke, on whose book *Science and Religion* I will now begin drawing, has said, "[I]t is almost impossible to exaggerate the extent to which belief in [divine] intervention once permeated European societies, creating popular images of the disruption of nature that could hardly have been congenial to a critical science of nature."[11]

What *is* surprising, given the centrality of miracles to the medieval Christian faith and the strongly supernaturalistic worldview built into the doctrine of *creatio ex nihilo*, is the degree to which some

---

*Several writers have suggested that science as we know it was dependent on the distinctive worldview that resulted from the synthesis of Greek and Hebrew ideas effected by medieval Christian thought. For example, Alfred North Whitehead famously suggested that the distinctive frame of mind that led to the uniquely European search for the secrets of nature must have come from "the medieval insistence on the rationality of God, conceived as with the personal energy of Jehovah and with the rationality of a Greek philosopher" (*Science and the Modern World*, 12).

Christians, once they were exposed to the naturalism of Aristotle and some of his Islamic commentators, tried to accommodate it. Already in the twelfth century, some Christian thinkers said that we need to refer to divine causation only for the original creation of the world, and that from then on virtually all things can be explained in terms of natural causes. The only exception would be the Christian miracles, in which God suspended the ordinary laws of nature in order to give testimony to Christianity as the true religion. Even this idea—that miracles are supernatural interruptions of the ordinary causal processes—was mitigated by the scheme of primary and secondary causation. According to this scheme, God is the *primary* cause of all events. Most events, however, are brought about indirectly by God, through natural causes, which are therefore called *secondary* causes. Miracles are simply events that God chose to bring about directly, without using secondary causes. They are not complete exceptions to the normal order, however, because God is the primary cause of *all* events.

Some thinkers in the twelfth and thirteenth centuries decided that their task, as natural philosophers, was to explain as much as they could in purely naturalistic terms, with a few of them even suggesting naturalistic explanations for some of the biblical miracles. The more radical of these philosophers said, under Aristotle's influence, that natural philosophy, employing only experience and reason, comes to conclusions that contradict Christian doctrines. Natural philosophy, in particular, was said to support the idea that the world is eternal, not created, that the soul is not immortal, that there are no miracles, including the resurrection of the body, and that there are certain things that God cannot do. On this last point, Christian theologians had always held that God could not do that which is logically contradictory, such as create round squares. But some of these Aristotelian philosophers, basing their claims on some things that Aristotle had considered impossible, such as a vacuum, said that there were certain things that, even though they involved no logical contradiction, God could not create.[12]

As these philosophers soon learned, there was a limit to what the church would tolerate. At the leading university at the time, Paris, propositions derived from Aristotle were condemned five times in the thirteenth century, with 219 propositions drawn from Aristotelian writings being forbidden in the famous condemnation of 1277. The most important of the forbidden propositions were those that taught that the world is eternal; that nature is a system of natural causes that is closed to divine providence and hence miracles; that there are some things, beyond logical contradictions, that God cannot do; and that there is no resurrection of the dead.[13] As this list shows, the issue involved was divine omnipotence and freedom over against the Aristotelian claim that our world embodies various necessary principles so that it could not, in some fundamental respects, be otherwise. In condemning this claim, says Lindberg, the church's spokesmen "declared, in opposition to Aristotle, that the world is whatever its omnipotent Creator chose to make it."[14]

At the root of this conflict was the question of whether the world was eternal or was created *ex nihilo*. Aristotle's position was based on the insight that the eternal and the necessary are identical: Whatever is eternal is necessary, and whatever is necessary is eternal. Combining this insight with the view that our world has always existed, Aristotle considered all the principles of our world—what later would be called the "laws of nature"—to be necessary. The Christian theologians, by contrast, held that not only our particular world but finitude itself was freely created by God out of absolute nothingness. Thomas Aquinas is representative. Thinking so highly of Aristotle that he referred to him simply as "the philosopher"— the one who had shown what reason would come to on its own, without the aid of supernatural revelation—Thomas agreed with him that reason could not prove that the world had a beginning. Holding, however, that this fact had been revealed, Thomas said, "According to our faith, nothing has always existed except God alone."[15]

Implicit in this doctrine, and emphasized by the condemnations more than by Thomas himself, was the idea that God, having freely created our world out of nothing, could have made it different in all respects and can now, in any case, interrupt any of the principles by which it normally operates.[16] This principle was brought out with absolute clarity by a nineteenth-century Calvinist theologian, Charles Hodge, who said in response to the question of how God is related to the laws of nature:

The answer to that question . . . is, First, that He is their author . . . .
Secondly, He is independent of them. He can change, annihilate, or
suspend them at pleasure. He can operate with or without them. The
"Reign of Law" must not be made to extend over Him who made the
laws.[17]

Hodge's statement illustrates the fact that there has been no form
of Christian theology that has emphasized the absolute freedom and
omnipotence of God more than Calvinism.

Although Calvinism did not appear until the sixteenth century,
mentioning it in connection with the thirteenth-century condemnations of Aristotelian ideas is not inappropriate, because these condemnations led in the fourteenth century to a preoccupation with the
theme of divine omnipotence, which provided the background for the
later emergence of Calvinism. The desire to emphasize the absolute
omnipotence of God without undercutting the kind of regularity presupposed by natural philosophy led to the distinction between the
absolute and the *ordained* power of God. "When we consider God's
power absolutely," explains Lindberg, summarizing this position,

> we acknowledge that God is omnipotent and can do as he wishes;
> at the moment of creation there were no factors other than the law
> of noncontradiction limiting the kind of world he might create. But
> in fact we recognize that God chose from among the infinity of pos-
> sibilities open to him and created *this* world; and, because he is a
> consistent God, we can be confident that he will (but for a rare
> exception) abide by the order thus established, and we need not
> worry about perpetual divine tinkering.[18]

For the most part, therefore, we can, according to this position, ignore
the absolute power of God, focusing only on the ordained power of
God, that is, God's decision to work, at least most of the time, through
the laws of this world.

Once this point had been established, the use of Aristotle to understand the contingent laws of this world was allowed. It came, in fact,
to be mandated. In 1323, Thomas Aquinas was elevated to sainthood,
a fact that helped his system become the most enduring synthesis of
biblical and Aristotelian thought. And beginning in 1341, teachers at
the University of Paris were required to swear that they would teach

"the system of Aristotle . . . , except in those cases that are contrary to the faith."[19] This slightly modified Aristotelian philosophy of nature would be dominant among natural philosophers until it was overthrown in the seventeenth century.

The distinction between the absolute and the ordained power of God represented a fourth major synthesis of biblical and Greek thought, sometimes called a synthesis of Jerusalem and Athens. The first synthesis had employed Plato's doctrine of creation out of chaos; the second synthesis involved a modification of Plato in the name of the doctrine of creation out of nothing; the third synthesis, paradigmatically effected by Thomas, involved Aristotle; while this fourth one, emphasizing the divine omnipotence and creation out of nothing, distanced itself from Greek philosophy more radically than had Thomas. The major difference was that whereas Thomas had emphasized the divine *reason*, saying that God acts on the basis of what God sees to be good, these fourteenth-century theologians emphasized the divine *will*, saying that there is nothing prior to the divine will that compromises the divine freedom, not even the idea of the good. Insofar as anything is good, it is so only because the divine will made it such. Given their emphasis on the freedom and priority of the divine will, these theologians are called "voluntarists." This voluntarist synthesis—by being embodied in both the Protestant Reformation and the Roman Catholic movement sometimes called the Counter-Reformation—would then lead in the seventeenth century to a fifth synthesis of biblical and Greek modes of thought, which can be called supernaturalistic mechanism.

4. Supernaturalistic Mechanism: The Early Modern Synthesis

This fifth synthesis, by virtue of becoming identified as the scientific worldview, is still of importance today, because its enduring legacy still determines to a considerable extent what can count in the scientific community as a "scientific explanation." Part of this enduring legacy is its mechanistic doctrine of nature. Whereas the previous syntheses of biblical and Greek thought had drawn primarily on Plato and Aristotle, this fifth one reached back to Democritus, according to whom everything is reducible to atoms moving in the void. However, these seventeenth-century thinkers—such as Marin Mersenne and René Descartes in the Catholic tradition and Robert Boyle and Isaac Newton in the Protestant—did not try to explain *everything* in these reductionist terms. The atoms, rather than moving randomly, were programmed by God, who had created the world *ex nihilo*. And, except for a few extremists such as Thomas Hobbes, these early modern thinkers did not try to explain human experience in terms of the collisions of atoms, but said that although the human body is a machine composed of material atoms, it is directed by a spiritual soul. The seventeenth-century synthesis, therefore, had a mechanistic doctrine of nature, a dualistic doctrine of the human being, and a supernaturalistic view of the universe as a whole.

Part of the occasion for this new synthesis was increasing unhappiness with the power that Aristotle's philosophy attributed to nature. The attack on Aristotle centered on his doctrine that the behavior of all natural things is influenced by "final causes," in the sense that their activity has a goal. This doctrine of final causation outraged those who had been nurtured by voluntarist theology. To regard the motion of things to be due partly to their own goal seeking, these voluntarists thought, was to attribute power to nature that really belonged to God.

In opposition to this view, Mersenne, Descartes, Boyle, and Newton developed what has aptly been called the "legal-mechanical view" of nature.[20] According to the "mechanical" part of this view, nature consists of lifeless bits of matter that operate entirely in terms of mechanical impact. Any activity that appears to be purposive is explained by the "legal" part of this doctrine, which says that all things move in terms of the laws of motion that God has imposed on the world. The language of "laws of nature," still used today by scientists whether they are theists or not, reflects this idea that the regularities of the world reflect divinely imposed laws. The laws of nature, said Descartes, are the "laws that God has put into nature." What we call "nature," said Boyle, is simply a "system of rules, according to which [the world's] agents, and the bodies they work on, are by the great Author of things, determined to act and suffer."[21]

Indeed, not only the laws of motion but the motion itself was derived from God. By emphasizing that the physical world is made of bits of matter in which motion is not inherent, these thinkers constructed a view of nature designed to carry through the idea implicit in the doctrine of *creatio ex nihilo*—that all power whatsoever belongs to God. The contrary idea underlying Greek naturalism—that explanations are to be made in terms of the inherent powers of nature—was completely eliminated. All principles and laws of nature, including motion and change of every sort, was now understood in terms of supernatural imposition.

The negative motivation behind this new synthesis was not, however, provided primarily by opposition to the Aristotelian philosophy of nature. As I have discussed in some detail elsewhere,[22] an even more important motive was the effort to defeat another naturalistic tradition, which had gained strength since emerging in the Neoplatonic renaissance of the fifteenth century. This third tradition, which involved a mixture of Neoplatonic, Hermetic, and Cabalistic ideas, is sometimes simply called the "magical" tradition because of its emphasis on influence at a distance. For example, Brian Easlea, describing its importance, says,

> "Modern science" emerged, at least in part, out of a three-cornered contest between proponents of the established [Aristotelian] view and adherents of newly prospering magical cosmologies, both to be opposed in the seventeenth century by advocates of revived mechanical world views. Scholastic Aristotelianism versus magic versus mechanical philosophies.[23]

For our purposes, the essential point is that this third tradition was a form of naturalism, which attributed even more power to nature than did Aristotelianism—not only the power of self-motion but also the power to exert and receive influence at a distance. We can call this tradition, therefore, "magical naturalism."

As to why the legal-mechanical view won out over this magical naturalism, the standard assumption has been that it simply offered better explanations. However, it is now commonplace among historians of the period to hold that, in Easlea's words, "the victory of this extraordinary [mechanical] philosophy over its equally extraordinary rival cannot be understood in terms of the relative explanatory successes of each basic cosmology but rather in terms of the fortunes of the social forces identified with each cosmology."[24]

This answer, in a nutshell, is that the legal-mechanical view won the battle of the worldviews because it seemed to support the social status quo, and thereby the interests of the rich and the powerful, whereas magical naturalism seemed to threaten those interests. In those days, the status quo was undergirded by the authority of the institutional church, which was believed to have the "keys to the kingdom" and thereby the power to determine the extramundane existence of human beings—whether they went to heaven or hell. The legal-mechanical view won largely because it was effectively put in service of a theology supportive of this church. I will illustrate this point by showing how the legal-mechanical view was used to defend the supernatural character of the Christian miracles, the immortality of the soul, and the existence of an omnipotent deity.

Miracles as Supernatural Interventions

The miracles of the New Testament had provided the main evidence that Christianity, alone among the religions of the world, had been ordained by God as *the* vehicle of ultimate truth and salvation.* Without the evidence of divine favor provided by supernatural attestations, the church's claim to possess the keys to the kingdom would have seemed groundless. This evidence would have been undermined if the events in question could have been given a naturalistic interpretation, and some representatives of magical naturalism, such as Thomas Fludd, were offering just that. Central to the claim that supernatural intervention was needed to explain the New Testament miracles, such as Jesus' healings, was the idea, supported by Aristotle, that the capacity to exert and receive influence at a distance is not a natural capacity. But Fludd argued that it is, adding that the miracles reported in the Bible were

---

*Robert Boyle, illustrating this view, said that "the miracles of Christ (especially his Resurrection) and those of his disciples, by being *works altogether supernatural*, . . .and being owned to be done in God's name, . . . authorize a doctrine . . . [because] he would [not] suffer such numerous, great miracles, to be set as his seals to a lie" (quoted in Brooke, *Science and Religion*, 134).

not different in kind from extraordinary events that have occurred in other traditions.[25]

Mersenne introduced the mechanical philosophy into France to answer this argument by Fludd, called by Mersenne the "principal enemy of Christian religion."[26] Fludd's position was so dangerous, Mersenne saw, because its view of what "nature" can do is so generous—allowing all sorts of marvels—that it provides no basis for drawing a clear line between the natural and the supernatural. Realizing that he needed an alternative system to defeat Fludd's philosophy, Mersenne appealed to Pierre Gassendi, who introduced him to the Democritean mechanistic philosophy, which had recently been revived in Italy by Galileo.[27] Mersenne could see that this view of "nature," which is even more restrictive than the Aristotelian view, denies the possibility of influence at a distance even more clearly, because it entails that one thing can influence another thing only by contact—by hitting it, as one billiard ball hits another. Mersenne enthusiastically adopted this mechanistic view, employing it to argue that, given a true understanding of "nature," the Christian miracles could not have occurred without supernatural intervention.[28] This Fludd-Mersenne debate was soon repeated in England, with Boyle using the mechanical philosophy against Henry Stubbe's naturalistic account of miracles.[29]

The Immortality of the Soul

Stubbe also used his naturalistic philosophy to affirm "mortalism," the doctrine that when your body dies so does your soul.[30] The main argument for the belief in the soul's immortality had been the Platonic idea that the soul, unlike the matter of which the body is composed, is self-moving. Given this difference in kind, the fact that the body decomposes at death provides no reason to think that the same fate awaits the soul. But from the perspective of magical naturalists such as Stubbe, the fact that the soul is a self-moving thing does not make it different from the body's components, because they are also self-moving entities. Stubbe used this argument to deny that those who rebel against the status quo have anything to fear after death for disobedience to the church. Boyle, employing the mechanistic view, argued that since the matter of which the body is composed is insentient and inert, our awareness of our consciousness and freedom proves that there must be something in us that is different in kind from matter, so it can be presumed not to share the fate of the material body. Therefore, Boyle argued, it would be foolish to ignore the question of rewards and punishment after bodily death.[31]

As an illustration of the effectiveness of this argument, we can point to the conversion of Walter Charleton to the mechanistic-dualistic view. Although Charleton had written several books espousing magical naturalism, he later turned his back on it, saying that its advocates were plotting "to murder *the immortality of the Soul* (the basis of all religion) and to deride the *Compensation of good and evil actions after death.*"[32] In favoring the mechanistic-dualistic view because of its support for immortality and thereby postmortem rewards and punishments, Charleton was following the argument of Descartes, the most famous advocate of the mechanistic-dualistic view. Having stated the status quo conviction that "present institutions are practically always more tolerable than would be a change in them," Descartes suggested that one of the main reasons people rebel against divinely appointed rulers is the assumption, based on the belief that the human soul is not different in kind from natural things, "that after the present life we have nothing to fear or to hope for, any more than flies or ants."[33]

An Omnipotent Deity

In renouncing magical naturalism, Charleton also denounced its advocates as atheists plotting to "undermine the received belief in an omnipotent *eternal being.*" If matter is self-moving, some of these advocates argued, then the world's order does not imply a transcendent source of order, because the world could be a self-organizing organism. The mechanistic view of matter as inert was also used to undermine that argument. As Boyle put it, "Since motion does not essentially belong to matter . . . , the motions of all bodies, at least at the beginnings of things, . . . were impressed upon them . . . by an external immaterial agent, God."[34]

Newton, besides accepting this argument for a First Mover,[35] also used the mechanistic view of matter to suggest a proof for a super-natural deity from the phenomenon with which Newton was most closely associated: gravitational attraction. Although Newton in his private work was very much involved in the magical tradition, pub-licly he distanced himself from it. Whereas magical naturalism regarded the power of mutual attraction as a natural capacity of mat-ter, Newton declared the idea that gravitation is "innate, inherent, and essential to matter" to be an "absurdity." Gravity, Newton added, "must be caused by an agent." Richard Bentley, having been coached by Newton on this point, wrote that "mutual gravitation or sponta-neous attraction can neither be inherent and essential to matter, nor ever supervene to it, unless impressed and infused into it by a divine power." Gravitation, concluded Bentley, provides "a new and invin-cible argument for the being of God."[36]

It was, to a great extent, through such arguments that the mecha-nistic doctrine of nature and the dualistic doctrine of the human soul, in the context of an extremely supernaturalistic view of deity, gained the allegiance of the elite members of the society in the latter part of the seventeenth century, especially those in position to determine the framework within which natural philosophy, or natural science, would be carried out.

5. From Supernaturalistic Dualism to Atheistic Materialism

Although the victory of a mechanical view of nature meant, in the eyes of its founders, a victory for a supernaturalistic, miracle-work-ing God and an immortal human soul, this victory was short-lived. Almost immediately, leading thinkers began making a transition to a naturalistic worldview that, while retaining the mechanistic view of nature, would discard God and the soul.

The first step in this process was, in Brooke's words, "a growing aversion among natural philosophers to talk of divine intervention."[37] This aversion produced a move toward a deistic view, according to which God, after creating the world with its motion and natural laws, did not intervene. Although this move toward deism was partly moti-vated by the problem of evil (which I will discuss in the next chapter), it was also partly motivated by the acceptance of a mechanistic, clockwork universe. Ironically, points out Brooke, this view of the universe, created by supernaturalists to support the belief in divine activity, quickly led to the conviction that the universe, once set it motion, could run on its own, with no further tinkering by the divine mechanic.[38] Boyle himself had said that nature

> is like a rare clock, such as may be that at Strasbourg, where all things are so skillfully contrived, that the engine being once set a moving, all things proceed, according to the artificer's first design, and the motions of the little statues, that at such hours perform these or those things, do not require, like those of puppets, the peculiar interposing of the artificer.[39]

Although Newton had pointed to several phenomena, such as the orbits of the planets, that seemed to him to require ongoing divine activity in the world, most natural philosophers found, as astronomer Pierre Laplace was alleged to have said, that they had "no need of that hypothesis." This deistic view constituted a sixth synthesis of Christian faith and the Greek naturalistic tradition.

At first the move toward deism was to a merely *virtual* deism, which allowed for a few divine interventions, perhaps only one. This position is illustrated by the famous geologist Charles Lyell, called the father of "uniformitarianism," which is the doctrine that in offering explanations of things in the past, we should not employ causes that are not operating today. We should, in other words, assume uniformity with regard to the world's causal processes. In spite of being damned by conservative Christians for espousing this doctrine, Lyell himself affirmed one exception. Believing that the origin of the human mind could not be explained in terms of natural causes alone, he suggested that divine intervention added "the moral and intellectual faculties of the human race, to a system of nature which had gone on for millions of years without the intervention of any analogous cause." This suggestion meant, Lyell acknowledged, that we must "assume a primeval creative power which does not act with uniformity."[40]

The transition from this virtual deism to complete deism can be observed in the change of mentality between Lyell and Charles Darwin, who had developed a theory of how humans could have evolved through natural selection of random variations. In a letter to his older friend, Darwin rejected the idea of divine additions to explain the distinctive capacities of the human mind: "I would give nothing for the theory of natural selection, if it requires miraculous additions at any one stage of descent."[41] Darwin still believed in a creator God, thinking evolution intelligible only on the assumption that God, in creating the universe, had built in laws of evolutionary development. But Darwin insisted on a consistently deistic view, with not a single interruption of these laws. As a member of a movement promoting what it called "scientific naturalism," Darwin saw this complete rejection of divine intervention as necessary for the fulfillment of this movement's ideal.

Nevertheless, the deistic view, even in its consistent form, was not completely naturalistic. By saying that the world was originally created *ex nihilo*, it implied that the basic principles of our world are not really *natural* in the sense of lying in the very nature of things. In principle, therefore, it was possible for these principles to be interrupted by their divine creator. This possibility, which stood in the way of a completely naturalistic worldview, was one of the reasons why Darwin's successors rejected his deism in favor of a completely atheistic worldview. *Neo*-Darwinism is an explicitly atheistic theory, devoted to showing how the evolutionary process, without any guidance whatsoever, could have produced the forms of life present in our world. Atheistic naturalism, more generally, has been the more-or-less official ideology of the scientific community for over a century. In this account, furthermore, I have focused on the English-speaking world, which made the transition to atheism slowly. In France, this transition had been made a century earlier. There this transition can be observed within the thought of a single person, Denis Diderot, arguably the most important figure of the French Enlightenment, who moved from dualistic deism to atheistic materialism between 1746 and 1749.*

As illustrated by Diderot, the move from supernaturalism to atheism was accompanied by a move from dualism to materialism, because the dualistic view of the mind-body relation could be defended only by an

---

*Diderot's rejection of deism was stated in 1749 in *The Letter on the Blind*. On the development of his atheism, see Buckley, *At the Origins of Modern Atheism*, 194–250.

appeal to supernatural causation. The idea that the mind or soul is different in kind from the body's components, used by Descartes to support its immortality, created the problem of how the two could interact. It *seems* that when I decide to raise my hand and then my hand goes up, my mind causes bodily motion by affecting my brain. But how is this conceivable? According to Descartes' conception, the brain's components, being part of the physical world, are spatially extended and operate entirely in terms of mechanical impact, analogous to the way billiard balls interact. The mind or soul, by contrast, is a purely spiritual substance. Not taking up space, it cannot collide with material things. As a being with freedom, the mind exercises final causation. How could two such completely different types of entities interact? Although Descartes talked about the pineal gland in this connection, that theory explained only *where* the interaction occurs, not *how*. With regard to that latter question, Descartes sometimes said that he did not know, but his real answer was that God, in creating the world, had ordained mind and body to interact.[42] This doctrine was more explicitly affirmed by the "occasionalists," who said that, given the absolute difference between soul and body, they could not possibly interact. Rather, on the occasion of your putting your hand on the hot stove, God causes your mind to feel pain; and then, on the occasion of your deciding to move your hand, God moves it for you.

As William James said, "For thinkers of that age, 'God' was the great solvent of all absurdities."[43] But, as we saw earlier, this appeal to God as a *deus ex machina* itself came to be perceived as absurd. Deists could still suppose that one of the things God had ordained in setting up the rules of the world is that mind and body would interact, or at least seem to. But once even this deistic form of supernaturalism was renounced, the problem of how mind and body, dualistically understood, could interact became intolerable, with Schopenhauer calling this problem "the world-knot."

Materialists decided to cut this knot by simply denying that what we call "the mind" refers to an entity distinct from the brain. The mind, some of them suggested, is simply a product of the brain, just as bile is a product of the liver—but a product that has no causal power of its own. Others suggested that the mind simply is the brain in one of its functionings—that just as the names "evening star" and "morning star" point to the same thing, so do the names "mind" and "brain." The mind and the brain, in other words, are said to be identical. Given this position, called *identism*, the question of how mind and brain can interact does not arise, because interaction presupposes two things. Nor does, of course, the question of whether human personality survives bodily death. Whereas mortalism was merely *allowed* by some of the early modern naturalists, it is *required* by late modern naturalism. This transition to materialism, occurring in the latter part of the nineteenth century in England, had occurred a century earlier in France, as illustrated not only by Diderot but also by a well-known book by Julien Offray de La Mettrie called *Man the Machine*, which appeared in 1747. As the title of that book suggests, the denial of dualism, in the context of a mechanistic view of nature and hence the human body, implied the denial of human freedom.*

This denial also implied the rejection of the possibility of life after death. This argument has been made by Corliss Lamont, for example, in a book called *The Illusion of Immortality*. The idea of life after bodily death is an illusion, he says, because the idea of the soul's immortality presupposed the dualistic view, whereas modern thought sees the mind as simply a function of the brain. Given this modern view, life after bodily death is "an impossibility."[44]

The seventeenth-century decision to employ the mechanistic doctrine of nature to support an immortal soul and a supernatural deity, and thereby to provide scientific support for a supernaturalistic version of Christian faith, had completely backfired. The mechanistic idea of nature instead led the scientific community, and thereby the intellectual community in general, to a naturalistic worldview that rejects not only miraculous interventions but also theism of any form, freedom, and life after death. The atheistic, materialistic version of naturalism is the seventh synthesis of Greek naturalism and Christian faith—with the latter represented only negatively.

---

*On the influence of Descartes on the development of French materialism, see Vartanian, *Diderot and Descartes*. As Vartanian shows, materialism as developed in Diderot, La Mettrie, and other French thinkers involved a more organismic form of mechanism, with an idea of matter as active, living, and creative. Their materialism, therefore, was not as obviously inadequate as that which developed later in the English-speaking world, which retained the fully mechanistic view of matter.

6. Scientific Naturalism in Distorted Form

Besides backfiring theologically, the forced marriage between mechanism and supernaturalism also resulted, after the divorce, in a form of naturalism that is inadequate for science. The transition to atheistic materialism did mean that supernaturalism, which had been introduced into the Western tradition by Christian theologians, had finally been overcome. Western science had finally returned to the naturalistic outlook, which had been introduced in Greece over two thousand years earlier. But it made this return in a very inadequate form. This late modern version of naturalism is, to be sure, associated with scientific knowledge of the world that makes the early Greek speculations look ridiculous. But *philosophically*, this late modern worldview is no more adequate than the views of Democritus and other earlier materialists, which both Plato and Aristotle had seen to be woefully inadequate.

In calling this late modern worldview inadequate, I am primarily employing the standard that I call "hard-core common sense." I add the adjective "hard-core" to distinguish this standard from the kind of ideas with which the term "common sense" is nowadays widely associated. These are ideas that are common only to people at a certain time and place, many of which turn out to be false. These ideas can be called "soft-core common sense." In referring to *hard*-core common sense, by contrast, I refer to various ideas that we *inevitably* presuppose in our practices, even if we deny them verbally.

An example is provided by our belief in the reality of a world beyond our own experience. The name for the denial of this belief is "solipsism." For me to profess to be a solipsist would be for me to claim that, for all I know, I am the only being that exists. The impossibility of living out this claim is illustrated by an old joke. After a philosopher announces in a lecture that he is a solipsist, a voice from the back of the room says, "Thank God! I was afraid I was the only one." The serious point here is that I could not assert my belief in solipsism without implicitly contradicting my assertion in the very act of making it. That is, in writing the assertion on my computer and then reading it in a lecture, I show that I know that computers, pieces of paper, and other people exist. In thereby implicitly affirming what my statement explicitly denies, I am both affirming and denying the same proposition. I am thereby violating the first rule of reason, the law of noncontradiction, which says that a proposition and its contradictory cannot both be true. Some philosophers call this violation a "performative self-contradiction," because the very performance of affirming the proposition contradicts its content.[45]

There are a number of our hard-core commonsense beliefs to which modern scientific naturalism cannot do justice. One of these is our belief that we have experience. As Descartes famously pointed out, there is at least one proposition that you cannot possibly doubt, which is that you, as a being with conscious experience, exist at this moment. To deny this—to say "I do not exist" or "I am not now conscious"—would involve a performative self-contradiction, because in saying "I" you would be implicitly affirming your present conscious existence.[46] However, as I have documented elsewhere,[47] materialist philosophers have been unable to explain how experience could have emerged out of the insentient (nonexperiencing) matter that they believe—as did the dualists of the seventeenth and eighteenth centuries—to constitute the bottom layer of nature. Although the rejection of dualism was supposed to make the mind-body problem go away, it did not. Materialists still face the problem of how a brain consisting of nonexperiencing neurons could produce conscious experience. The most candid of the materialist philosophers, furthermore, admit that they cannot solve this problem. Colin McGinn, for example, says that we have no understanding of how "the aggregation of millions of individually insentient neurons [constituting the brain] generate subjective awareness."[48]

The other side of the mind-body problem is how our conscious experience can affect the brain and thereby bring about bodily behavior. This is the problem of "mental causation." None of us in practice doubts that such causation occurs. As philosopher Jaegwon Kim says, we know that our decision to make a phone call causes us to walk to the phone and dial it.[49] No one can consistently deny the reality of mental causation. If I said, "Read my lips—no bodily behavior is produced by thoughts," my use of my lips to make this statement would constitute a performative contradiction. Yet, although the reality of mental causation cannot be consistently doubted, materialists have been unable to explain how it could occur. After working on the problem for some twenty years, Jaegwon Kim, deciding that it could not be solved, said that he and his fellow materialists seem to be "up against a dead end."[50]

Closely related to the problem of mental causation is the issue of human freedom. We all presuppose that we and other people have a degree of freedom, so that we are partly responsible for our behavior. We show that we presuppose this every time we blame other people for their actions or suffer guilt feelings for our own. Philosophers who accept the mechanistic-materialistic view of human beings, however, have been unable to explain how human freedom is possible. Regarding the mind as identical with the brain, which is simply a very complex part of the physical world, they have to conclude that human beings have no more freedom than billiard balls and computers.

Philosopher John Searle, while endorsing materialism, has been especially forthright about its inability to account for freedom. Science, says Searle, "allows no place for freedom of the will," because science teaches that the world "consists entirely of mindless, meaningless, physical particles."[51] Any indeterminacy in these particles at the quantum level, Searle points out, does not help, because it is canceled out in large aggregations of them, such as rocks, computers, and human bodies.[52] The fact that the scientific worldview rules out freedom creates a real problem, Searle acknowledges, because "we can't act otherwise than on the assumption of freedom, no matter how much we learn about how the world works as a determined physical system."[53] Searle thereby points out that the belief in freedom is a hard-core commonsense belief. Although he concludes that our assumption of freedom must be an illusion, Searle acknowledges that he cannot help believing that he reached this conclusion freely. This is one of the paradoxes to which the present version of scientific naturalism leads.

This form of naturalism also cannot account for our mathematical knowledge. My previous discussion did not prepare the way for this problem, so I must return to the seventeenth century momentarily. In rejecting magical naturalism, part of what thinkers such as Descartes and Boyle were rejecting was its view of knowledge, which allowed for *nonsensory* perception. One problem with belief in nonsensory perception was that it allowed people to believe that they could have a direct experience of God—which was called "enthusiasm" (the word "enthused," of course, literally means "filled with God"). Enthusiasts created a social problem, because they often believed that they had revelations that superseded the teachings of the established church. Another problem with belief in nonsensory perception was that it allowed for telepathy, which literally means "feeling at a distance." If telepathy were a natural capacity, they saw, then the so-called mental miracles of Jesus, such as his knowing what was in the mind of the woman at the well, would not have required supernatural powers. And this is precisely what some of the advocates of magical naturalism held.

Partly to rule out this interpretation as well as to discredit enthusiasm, the defenders of orthodoxy rejected the possibility of nonsensory perception by affirming the *sensationist doctrine of perception.* According to sensationism, all perception comes through our physical senses. With the help of the philosophies of John Locke, David Hume, and Immanuel Kant, this sensationist doctrine of perception became a dogma of modern thought. It is the other doctrine from the seventeenth century, along with the mechanistic view of nature, that is retained by today's scientific naturalism.

This retention of sensationism has created enormous problems, one of which is how knowledge of mathematical objects is possible. Mathematics has been central to modern science ever since the time of Kepler and Galileo, who, as modern Pythagoreans, declared mathematics to be the language God used to write the "Book of Nature." It would be a very serious matter, therefore, if scientific naturalists could not explain how human beings can do mathematics. And currently they cannot. The problem is created by the fact that our physical senses are activated only by physical things, while mathematical objects are not physical things but eternal forms, which, as Plato said, the mind can know only through nonsensory intuition. In rejecting a mind distinct from the brain, however, today's scientific naturalism rules out the possibility of any such intuition. As Harvard philosopher Hilary Putnam has put it, "we think with our brains, and not with immaterial souls." Therefore, he concluded, "We cannot envisage *any* kind of neural process that could . . . correspond to the 'perception of a mathematical object.'"* The seriousness of this problem is shown by the fact that it constitutes virtually the entire subject of the subdiscipline known as the philosophy of mathematics. The impossibility of solving it within the present form of naturalism is shown by the fact that the dominant responses have been either simply to ignore the problem, which is now Putnam's approach,† or to deny that numbers exist, which is exemplified in books with titles such as *Science without Numbers* and *Mathematics without Numbers.*[54]

For these and still other reasons, scientific naturalism in its present form is, besides being incompatible with religious belief, wholly inadequate for science itself. I call this doctrine naturalism$_{sam}$, with "sam" standing for sensationist-atheistic-materialistic. I do believe that naturalism$_{ns}$, which simply rejects supernatural interruptions, is a great truth. But by becoming embodied in a great falsehood, naturalism$_{sam}$, this great truth has appeared in our time in a grossly distorted form.

In the next chapter, I will describe how Christian faith, another great truth, became equally distorted, becoming a great falsehood. In the third and fourth chapters, I will discuss a new form of naturalism, which can serve equally for the scientific and the Christian communities.

NOTES

1. Cobb, *Beyond Dialogue*, x.
2. I have sought to do this in my *Religion and Scientific Naturalism*.
3. Whitehead, *Science and the Modern World*, 5, 12.
4. Lindberg, *The Beginnings of Western Science*, 24.
5. Ibid., 26.
6. Ibid., 26, 27.
7. Ibid., 42–43.
8. Ibid., 39, 43.

---

*Putnam, *Words and Life*, 503. Putnam was responding to Kurt Gödel's suggestion that we know mathematical objects through a nonsensory kind of perception. This suggestion was also derisively rejected in Chihara, "A Gödelian Thesis regarding Mathematical Objects: Do They Exist? And Can We Perceive Them?"

†Having said of his Harvard colleague Willard Quine that he simply "ignores the problem as to how we can know that abstract entities exist unless we can interact with them in some way," Putnam himself came to endorse this view (Putnam, *Words and Life*, 153, 156).

9. Ibid., 151–57, 208–13.

10. Ibid., 157, 174–75, 208–13.

11. Brooke, *Science and Religion*, 44.

12. Lindberg, *The Beginnings of Western Science*, 197–201, 234–35.

13. Ibid., 236–38.

14. Ibid., 239.

15. Quoted in Brooke, *Science and Religion*, 60.

16. Lindberg, *The Beginnings of Western Science*, 242.

17. Hodge, *Systematic Theology*, 1:607.

18. Lindberg, *The Beginnings of Western Science*, 243.

19. Ibid., 241.

20. See Klaaren, *The Religious Origins of Modern Science*.

21. Descartes and Boyle are quoted in Brooke, *Science and Religion*, 19 and 132, respectively.

22. Griffin, *Religion and Scientific Naturalism*, chap. 5.

23. Easlea, *Witch Hunting, Magic and the New Philosophy*, 89.

24. Ibid., 89–90.

25. Ibid., 94–95.

26. Quoted in Crombie, "Marin Mersenne," 317.

27. Easlea, *Witch Hunting, Magic and the New Philosophy*, 108.

28. Lenoble, *Mersenne ou la naissance du méchanisme*, 133, 157–58, 375, 381.

29. Easlea, *Witch Hunting, Magic and the New Philosophy*, 94–95.

30. See Jacob, "Boyle's Atomism and the Restoration Assault," 218–19, and Mosse, "Puritan Radicalism and the Enlightenment."

31. See Jacob, *Robert Boyle and the English Revolution*, 161–76.

32. Quoted in Easlea, *Witch Hunting, Magic and the New Philosophy*, 135.

33. Cottingham et al., eds., *Philosophical Writings of Descartes*, 1:46.

34. *The Works of the Honourable Robert Boyle*, 4:394.

35. Newton's argument for a First Mover is given in Koyré, *From the Closed World to the Infinite Universe*, 216.

36. Bentley's Newtonian argument is given in Koyré, *From the Closed World*, 178–79, 183, 184.

37. Brooke, *Science and Religion*, 155.

38. Ibid., 13, 118, 136, 140.

39. *The Works of the Honourable Robert Boyle*, 5:163. This passage is quoted by Baumer, *Religion and the Rise of Scepticism*, at the outset of the chapter on the seventeenth century, which is entitled "The Strasbourg Clock."

40. Lyell's statements are quoted in Hooykaas, *Natural Law and Divine Miracle*, 114.

41. Francis Darwin, ed., *The Life and Letters of Charles Darwin*, 2:6–7.

42. See Baker and Morris, *Descartes' Dualism*, 167–70.

43. James, *Some Problems of Philosophy*, 195.

44. Lamont, *The Illusion of Immortality*, 86, 123, viii.

45. See Jay, "The Debate over Performative Contradiction."

46. That this point was implicit in Descartes' argument is pointed out in Jaakko Hintikka, "Cogito, Ergo Sum. Inference or Performance."

47. Griffin, *Unsnarling the World-Knot*, chap. 6; *Religion and Scientific Naturalism*, chap. 6.

48. McGinn, *The Problem of Consciousness*, 1.

49. Kim, *Supervenience and Mind*, 286.

50. Ibid., 367. Chapter 10 of my *Unsnarling the World-Knot* is devoted to a critique of Kim's position. This critique is reprinted, in slightly revised form, as "Materialist and Panexperientialist Physicalism: A Critique of Jaegwon Kim's *Supervenience and Mind*," in *Process Studies* 28/1–2 (spring-summer 1999), followed by a response by Kim and a rejoinder from me.

51. Searle, *Minds, Brains, and Science*, 92, 13.

52. Ibid., 86–87.

53. Ibid., 86, 97.

54. Field, *Science without Numbers*; Hellman, *Mathematics without Numbers*.

Chapter 2

Christian Faith

A Great Truth That Got Distorted

*H*aving in the previous chapter argued that scientific naturalism is a great truth that got distorted, I will in this chapter suggest the same with regard to Christian faith, putting equal emphasis on the truth and the distortion. Some critics of Christianity, focusing on its distortions, deny, whether explicitly or only implicitly, that it contains any deep truth, while many of Christianity's defenders, emphasizing its truth, ignore or even deny any great distortions. To me, both the truth and the distortions seem equally real. I will begin by summarizing what I take to be the great truth of Christian faith.

1. Primary Doctrines of the Christian Good News

In speaking of Christian faith as true, I am referring to the *content* of faith—what was traditionally called *fides quae creditur*, the faith that is believed (as distinct from *fides qua creditur*, faith as believing, or the act of faith). We should think of the content of Christian faith, I suggest, as what can be called the primary doctrines of the Christian gospel, or good news. A summary of the Christian good news, in my view, would include the following doctrines:

1. *Our world has been created by a good, loving, wise, purposive God.** This part of the Christian good news stands in contrast with

---

*For convenience, I here follow the practice, which is widespread in Christian circles even if grammatically questionable, of using the word "God," capitalized, as both a designator of a type of being (a god) and a personal name for the divine being in which we believe.

doctrines that have maintained that our world was not created at all but has existed eternally, or that it was created by an evil power, an indifferent power, or a power devoid of intelligence and purpose.

2. *God, loving all of us, desires that we treat each other with justice and compassion.* This doctrine stands in contrast with all philosophies holding that human morality is *purely* human, not rooted in the nature of the universe. As creator of our universe, God is obviously the ultimate power of the universe. Since we as religious beings want to be in harmony with the ultimate power of the universe, these first two doctrines provide a basis for Christian morality.

3. *Our world is essentially good, even though it is now full of evil.* This doctrine stands in contrast with Manichean, gnostic doctrines, which consider the world to be essentially evil, and with doctrines that regard the world as neutral in the sense of being entirely "beyond good and evil."

4. *God continues to act in the world, especially through human beings, to foster good and overcome evil.* This doctrine stands in contrast with deistic views, according to which we are now on our own.

5. *God's love, concern for justice, and purpose, having already been expressed through a series of prophets and sages, were revealed in a decisive way through Jesus of Nazareth.* This doctrine stands in contrast with all views holding that if there is any divine influence in the world, it is a constant, nonvariable influence, so that no event can be more revelatory of the divine character and purpose than any other event.

6. *The divine purpose, thus revealed, is to overcome evil by bringing about a "reign of God" on earth, in which the present subjugation of life to demonic values (lies, ugliness, injustice, hate, and indifference) will be replaced by a mode of life based on divine values (truth, beauty, goodness, justice, and compassion).* This doctrine stands in contrast with the view that we cannot expect any fundamental change for the better in the nature of civilization, and also with the view that God's saving purpose is only to rescue us from this wicked world, not to overcome its wickedness.

7. *Salvation can be enjoyed here and now, at least in a partial way, through direct experience of, and empowerment by, God as Holy Spirit, and by the faith that, no matter what, our lives have ultimate*

meaning, because nothing can separate us from the love of God. This doctrine stands in contrast with all views that delay salvation entirely to a future state, whether on this earth or beyond.

8. *The divine purpose is also to bring about an even more complete salvation in a life beyond bodily death.* This doctrine stands in contrast with the view that the only salvation, or wholeness, that we will experience is what we experience in this life—a doctrine that would mean that the Christian "gospel" would *not* be good news to most people.

These eight doctrines, each one of which, if true, is clearly "good news," summarize my own understanding of the Christian gospel. Other theologians would, of course, come up with a more-or-less different summary. Still others, regarding Christianity more as a trajectory than a set of beliefs, reject the attempt to point to some "essence of Christianity" that has remained the same—or even could and should have remained the same—down through the centuries. It seems to me, however, that all Christian theologians presuppose, even if they have not brought this presupposition to clear consciousness, that there are certain ideas, which they share with the Bible, that are essential to authentic Christian faith, as distinct from historic doctrines that are optional to, or even distortions of, this faith. In any case, if we are to suggest that Christian faith is true, it is incumbent upon us to state just what it is that we claim to be true. This summary of primary doctrines of the Christian good news is my attempt to do this.

In calling them *primary* doctrines, I am distinguishing them from *secondary* doctrines, which have been developed to support certain primary doctrines, and *tertiary* doctrines, which have been developed to support particular secondary doctrines. An example of a secondary doctrine is that of the virgin birth of Jesus. The primary doctrine it was intended to support is the doctrine that God's activity in and through Jesus resulted in God's character and purpose being revealed in a decisive way. The doctrine that Jesus' mother was impregnated by God as Holy Spirit, rather than by a man, was one way of trying to explain the special relationship between God and Jesus. Later, after the emergence of Augustine's doctrine of original sin—according to which all babies are born in a state of sin, inheriting it from their parents—the doctrine of the virgin birth was used to explain why this was not true of Jesus, who, according to the Letter to the Hebrews, was like the rest of us except for being without sin. Of course, this doctrine of the virgin birth took care of only half the problem, namely, the Joseph half. The other half was handled by the development of a tertiary doctrine, that of Mary's "immaculate conception."

A more complete analysis would get quite complex. Augustine's doctrine of original sin, for example, was a secondary doctrine, being a particular way of formulating what it is that Jesus saves us from. Hebrews' statement that Jesus was without sin was itself a secondary doctrine, attempting to state how Jesus' relationship to God was special. In being used to reconcile these two secondary doctrines, the virgin birth, originally a secondary doctrine, became a tertiary doctrine. The immaculate conception, therefore, was really a fourth-level doctrine. For our purposes, however, we can ignore this additional complexity, limiting our attention to the distinction between primary doctrines, on the one hand, and doctrines that are secondary or tertiary, on the other hand, using "tertiary" to stand for all doctrines intended to support a secondary doctrine, even those that are in reality fourth- or even fifth-level doctrines.

This distinction between primary and nonprimary doctrines is essential if we are to argue for the truth of the Christian faith, because many of the secondary and tertiary doctrines that have been developed are clearly false, or at least highly dubious. Many people who reject Christian faith as false, even superstitious, have in mind such doctrines. For example, when the pastor in one of Ingmar Bergman's films, looking at the crucified Jesus on the cross, says, "Absurd," he surely has in mind various doctrines that, whatever one thinks about their truth, are secondary or tertiary. One could hold that those doctrines are false while still accepting the truth of Christianity's primary doctrines.

2. Some Early Distortions of Christian Faith

Having summarized the set of doctrines that I consider the great truth offered by the Christian faith, I turn now to a consideration of some of the ways it has been distorted. One basic way was implicit in the previous discussion.* That is, secondary or even tertiary doctrines have often been presented as if they were essential parts of the Christian gospel. This problem has occurred over and over because of the phenomenon that can be called "reverence by association." A secondary doctrine, seen at a particular time and place as necessary to safeguard a primary doctrine, comes to be perceived with the same reverence as the primary doctrine itself. Then a tertiary doctrine, seen at a particular time and place as necessary to protect that secondary doctrine, comes to be perceived with equal reverence. It has often become difficult, therefore, for Christians, unaware of the contingent circumstances in which these secondary and tertiary doctrines were created, to distinguish between the primary doctrines of their faith and the entire set of doctrines they have received from the tradition.

Such developments are especially distorting if these secondary or tertiary doctrines are either mythological or simply false. In saying this, I am presupposing that historic Christian doctrines can be divided into three categories: those that are rather literally true, such as those in my list of primary doctrines; those that express a truth but in mythological form; and those that are simply false.

Many of the historic doctrines can be considered true if and only if they are regarded as mythological in form rather than as literally true. The doctrine of "the fall" provides a good example. If taken literally, the story—involving the serpent (understood to be the devil), Adam and Eve as an actual couple, the inheritance of their sin by future generations through biological procreation, the inheritance also of their guilt, so that all of humankind stands under condemnation until absolved through the act of the "second Adam"—is simply nonsense. But if taken, as Reinhold Niebuhr suggested myths should

---

*In speaking of "one basic way," I thereby signal the fact this is not the only basic way. Another one, which lies beyond the scope of this book, involves a change of emphasis, or even a reversal, of the original Christian message. Examples would include the change of emphasis from Jesus' own message, involving a reign of God on earth, to a focus on Jesus himself, with his death and resurrection regarded as more important than his message (for an early critique of this transformation, see Rauschenbusch, *A Theology for the Social Gospel*); the change from the egalitarianism of the Jesus movement, in which women played a central role, to an increasing conformity to patriarchy (see Pagels, *The Gnostic Gospels,* and Schüssler Fiorenza, *In Memory of Her*); and the development of an anti-Judaistic theology (see Ruether, *Faith and Fratricide*, and Williamson, *Has God Rejected His People?*).

be taken, seriously but not literally,[1] the story conveys a deep truth. This truth is that although the world is essentially good and although human beings lived for a long time in what would, compared with later conditions, be recalled as a state of paradise, human existence did, only a few thousand years ago with the rise of civilization, suffer a fall into an alienated state. In this alienated state, the relative harmony of previous human communities was replaced by a mode of existence involving war, patriarchy, slavery, destruction of the environment, and a division between the rich and the poor, with the former oppressing the latter.[2] This state of sin is inherited—more socially than biologically—as the institutions, privileges, attitudes, ideologies, and habits that perpetuate this alienated state are passed on from generation to generation.

The idea of Satan, or the devil, which plays an essential role in the Christian story of the fall, can also be regarded as the mythological expression of a deep truth. Taken literally, the idea of Satan—as a personal, all-knowing, ubiquitous being who rivals God in power, and who presides over a hoard of demons (the original Evil Empire)—is surely false. No mere creature could approximate the divine power, let alone be omnipresent and omniscient. Taken as a mythological formulation, however, the idea of a demonic power of universal scope expresses a deep truth, one that the church in our time needs to make central to its understanding of its mission. This is the idea that human civilization, and thereby each of us within it, is now under subjugation to demonic power. In speaking of demonic power, I mean power that is diametrically opposed to our creator's purposes and is sufficiently powerful to thwart these purposes.[3] In the grip of ideologies and institutions of death and destruction, human civilization now has multiple ways of destroying itself, along with most of the rest of the life of the planet, thereby destroying myriad beautiful forms of life that it has taken God billions of years to foster.

The ideas of Satan and the fall can be regarded, therefore, as mythological expressions of deep truths. Countless people, however, have been led to reject Christian doctrine as false because they were told that these ideas, along with many other doctrines that are mythological in form, had to be accepted literally.

Besides such doctrines, which are false only if taken literally, there are some historic doctrines that, we should frankly admit, are simply false. As one who accepts the reality of paranormal occurrences,* however, my list of such doctrines is somewhat shorter than that of some of my fellow theologians, since there are fewer things that I consider absolutely impossible. I do not, for example, rule out the possibility that some of the miracle stories, such as those involving healings and the multiplication of food, are based on actual occurrences.† However, the category of doctrines that are simply false includes, I strongly suspect, at least some of the doctrines involving miracles, such as the doctrine of the virgin birth of Jesus. The doctrine of the perpetual virginity of Mary seems even more clearly to be false, especially given the fact that the New Testament speaks freely of Jesus' siblings.

Although such doctrines distort Christian faith simply by their falsity—if they are indeed false—the more serious distortion occurs when they are treated as if they were primary doctrines. This distortion occurred in the fundamentalist movement in America in the early decades of the twentieth century, in which the doctrine of the virgin birth was one of five doctrines used as the test of true Christians. This doctrine was often in effect treated as more important than the primary doctrines, insofar as the question of whether one accepted the virgin birth seemed more crucial to determining whether one was a true Christian than, say, the doctrines that God loves us all and wants us to treat each other with compassion.

In any case, having distinguished between doctrines that are true only mythologically and those that are simply false, I now add that there are some doctrines that arguably could be classified either way. The idea of Jesus as "the son of God" provides an example. On the one hand, the idea that Jesus was in some sense simply God— in particular, that Jesus was the incarnation of the second person of

---

*For a discussion of the philosophical possibility of, and empirical evidence for, such occurrences, see my *Parapsychology, Philosophy, and Spirituality*.

†See Murphy, *The Future of the Body*, and McClenon, *Wondrous Events*. These studies, along with the evidence supplied by parapsychology (see the previous footnote), suggest that such events have occurred in all times and places, thereby lending support to the view of the "magical naturalists," discussed in the first chapter, that such events, while perhaps extraordinary (parapsychologists call them "paranormal"; Murphy prefers "metanormal") are not supernatural.

the Divine Trinity in such a way that Jesus shared in the divine omniscience—should be discarded as simply false. Insofar as the formula of Chalcedon meant to say that Jesus was "fully divine" in this sense and yet also "fully human," it was, as countless critics have pointed out, self-contradictory. Since it belongs to the definition of a human being to be finite in knowledge, it is impossible for a being to be fully human and yet omniscient. The idea of Jesus as the son of God in this sense should be rejected as simply false. On the other hand, one could claim that this idea gives poetic or mythological expression to a deep truth about Jesus, which is that God was present in him and acted through him in an extraordinary way. I myself accept this idea, partly because in my view of the God-world relation, God does—contrary to those who reject all "enthusiasm"—influence us by, in one sense, entering into us. However, given the fact that the language of Jesus as the son of God so widely suggests the idea that he was God the Son, it seems better to place this doctrine in the category of the simply false. My conviction about this is reinforced when I recall the close association between this doctrine and the doctrine of Mary as "Theotokos," meaning "God-bearer" and hence "Mother of God." If the idea that a woman could give birth to God is not to be put in the category of the simply false, what should be?

In any case, the category of the simply false should not be thought to be limited to doctrines involving incredible events. There are many other doctrines taught in earlier centuries that we now consider, or at least should consider, false. Some of these are doctrines that reflected the science of the time but have later been shown to be false. Among these would be the doctrine of a three-storied universe, with heaven literally (spatially) above us and hell below; the geocentric idea that our planet is the center of the universe; the doctrine that our world was created only a few thousand years ago; and the idea that all the present species were created by God directly and virtually all at once, rather than through a long evolutionary process. Whereas these doctrines were disproved by advances in the *natural* sciences, other ones—such as the doctrine that the first five books of the Bible were written by one person, Moses—have been disproved by advances in the *historical* sciences.

There are still other doctrines that at least many of us have consigned to the category of the simply false, even though they do not involve either self-contradictions, improbable events, or outdated science. Among such doctrines I would include the idea of hell as a divinely created place of everlasting torment; the idea that there is no salvation outside the church, so that all or at least most people who do not accept the Christian faith will end up in hell; and the idea that God has predestined some people to heaven, others to hell. If pressed as to exactly why I consider these ideas false, part of the answer would be that I simply consider them, frankly, incredible. Another answer many would give is that they find them simply too horrible to be true. Although this answer might be criticized as wishful thinking—after all, many accounts of horrible things *are* true—this answer is actually a good one for Christians to give. At the very center of our faith is the affirmation that our world is essentially good because it has been created by a good and loving creator. If this affirmation is not contradicted by the doctrines of hell, damnation for those outside the church, and double predestination, what *could* contradict it?

With these doctrines, we have come to the worst way in which Christian faith has been distorted by some secondary and tertiary doctrines—namely, when such doctrines undermine the primary doctrines, thereby turning the Christian good news into very bad news. I turn now to what I consider the most important of such doctrines—one that was already discussed in the previous chapter—the doctrine of creation out of nothing.

3. The Major Distortion: *Creatio ex Nihilo*

Although it is widely assumed that the doctrine of *creatio ex nihilo* is biblical, this view is now rejected by leading scholars. The most thorough treatments are found in Jon Levenson's *Creation and the Persistence of Evil* and Gerhard May's *Creatio Ex Nihilo*.

Levenson, arguing that the doctrine of *creatio ex nihilo* is "post-biblical," says that the opening chapter of the book of Genesis, properly understood, "cannot be invoked in support of the . . . doctrine of *creatio ex nihilo*."[4] The belief that it does support that doctrine has been based on the fact that the opening verses have been translated to read, "In the beginning God created the heaven and the earth. The earth was without form and void." But that translation, Levenson points out, creates problems. One problem is that the verse thereby suggests that the heaven and the earth were created at the very beginning, but later verses say that they were created on the second and third days, respectively.[5] This inconsistency is removed if the first two verses are translated, as they now are by most scholars of the Hebrew Bible, as "When God began to create the heaven and the earth, the world was without form and void."[6] On this reading, God created our world out of a primeval chaos. Another count against the idea that Genesis 1 implies *creatio ex nihilo* is the fact that there is no mention of the waters and the darkness having been created, which suggests that they belonged to the primeval chaos.[7]

These alternative ways of understanding the origin of our universe suggest different conceptions of divine power. The idea that God created our universe out of a chaotic state opens up the possibility that the "material" from which our world was created had some power of its own, so that it was not wholly subject to the divine will. Plato, we recall, explicitly made this point, saying that the creator willed that everything should be good "as far as possible."[8] The contrary idea, that our universe was created out of complete nothingness, suggests that the divine creator is absolutely omnipotent. The attempt to read the beginning of Genesis as endorsing this view, in spite of its reference to a formless void, has usually involved a "two-stage" theory, according to which God first created the raw material out of nothing, then used it to create our world. This view implies that the basic elements of the world, owing their existence wholly to the creator's will, have no inherent power with which to offer any resistance to that will. This understanding is expressed by Millard Erickson, a contemporary Calvinist theologian: "God did not work with something which was in existence. He brought into existence the very raw material which he employed. If this were not the case, God would . . . have been limited by having to work with the intrinsic characteristics of the raw material which he employed."[9]

This understanding of the importance of the difference between the two readings is supported by Levenson. The revised reading is important, he says, because the assumption that the Hebrews believed in *creatio ex nihilo* has led to the distorted view that they thought of God as in complete control of all the forces of the universe.[10] This view is a distortion because not only the first chapter of Genesis but also most of the other relevant passages in the Hebrew Bible, says Levenson, indicate that our ordered world came into being only after God had defeated a primordial source of chaos.[11] The title of Levenson's book, *Creation and the Persistence of Evil*, points to the fact that the Hebrews believed that chaos had only been circumscribed, not annihilated, with the result that it constantly threatens to erupt.[12] The interpretation of the Hebrew Bible as teaching *creatio ex nihilo*, says Levenson, has become "the cornerstone of an overly optimistic undestanding of the theology of the Hebrew Bible."[13] Had the Hebrews thought of God as in complete control, they would have had to consider the persistence of evil a complete mystery—or else conclude that this world's creator is less than perfectly good.

Gerhard May's book, besides also pointing out that the doctrine of *creatio ex nihilo* is nowhere to be found in the Hebrew Bible, adds that it is also not found in the intertestamental literature or the New Testament. The main evidence for its presence in intertestamental Judaism has always been 2 Maccabees 7:28, which says that God created the world and humanity "out of nonbeing." May points out, however, that this formula does not necessarily imply *creatio ex nihilo* in the strict sense, according to which the very stuff of which this world is composed was itself created out of nothing.[14] In the fourth century B.C., for example, the Greek philosopher Xenophon said that parents "bring forth their children out of nonbeing," and in the first century A.D., the Hellenistic Jewish philosopher Philo spoke of God as creating "out of nonbeing," even though Philo accepted the existence of a preexistent matter alongside God.[15] The formula *creatio ex nihilo*, in other words, was simply an "unreflective, everyday way of saying that through the act of creation something arose which did not previously exist." As such, it did not imply the doctrine of *creatio ex nihilo* in the strict sense.[16]

The lack of evidence for this doctrine in pre-Christian Judaism undermines, in turn, the argument that there is evidence for it in the New Testament. This argument was based on the view, May points out, that "primitive Christianity found the doctrine ready-made in the Jewish tradition," so that "[o]ne would be able to presuppose it for the New Testament."[17] On this basis, New Testament scholars have traditionally argued that passages such as John 1:3, Romans 4:17, Colossians 1:16, and Hebrew 11:3, while not explicitly endorsing the doctrine of *creatio ex nihilo*, can safely be taken as allusions to it. May, having undermined this argument by showing that there is no evidence that the doctrine existed in the prior Jewish tradition, then argues that neither these passages, nor any other passages in the New Testament, provide evidence for it.[18] May's testimony is especially important because he himself, as a Christian theologian, accepts the doctrine of *creatio ex nihilo*, so he cannot be suspected of slanting the historical evidence to support his own position.

Besides the fact that there is no evidence of the doctrine of *creatio ex nihilo* during the first Christian century, when the New Testament was being written, there is also no evidence for it during most of the second century. Instead, Christian theologians typically reflected the position of Middle Platonism, according to which, although the *ordered* cosmos originated in time, unformed matter—along with the Platonic forms—is coeternal with God.[19] May points out that many second-century theologians considered "orthodox" by later standards, including Justin Martyr, Athenagoras, and Clement of Alexandria, held that the "acceptance of an unformed matter was entirely reconcilable with biblical monotheism."[20] In fact, Justin so thoroughly presupposed that this was what the Bible taught that he argued that Plato plagiarized Moses, borrowing "the doctrine that God made the cosmos out of unoriginate matter from the opening verses of Genesis."[21] So, although Thomas Aquinas and other medieval theologians assumed that the doctrine of *creatio ex nihilo* had been divinely revealed, these earlier theologians obviously did not think so. Why then did the doctrine arise?

The answer, May shows, is that it arose as a response to the threat to the (primary) doctrine of the essential goodness of our world raised by Marcion's gnostic theology.[22] According to this theology, our world is filled with evil because it was formed out of evil matter by the Hebrew Bible's creator God, who, Marcion held, is an evil deity, different from the supreme God revealed in Jesus.[23] Historians of

Christianity have long known that Marcion was responsible, in a negative way, for the creation of the New Testament canon. That is, only after Marcion had put together a collection of Christian writings, intended to support his heretical position, did the church settle on a set of Christian writings considered divinely inspired, which thereby became Scripture. May's account shows that Marcion was also responsible, again in a negative way, for the emergence of the doctrine of *creatio ex nihilo*.

Many Christian theologians, as we have seen, had accepted the eternity of matter. But Marcion, besides accepting that idea, also regarded this matter as evil. By saying that our world was created out of evil matter, Marcion contradicted the conviction of Christian faith that the world is essentially good—that insofar as it is now evil, it is so only contingently. A few Christian theologians decided that the best way to meet this threat was to reject the idea that matter is eternal, affirming instead that our world was created out of absolutely nothing. This need not have been the response. Marcion's idea was actually incoherent. According to the Platonic doctrine in question, our world was created out of *unformed* matter. Being unformed, it was devoid of any character, and hence was neither good nor evil but simply neutral.[24] Christian theologians could have responded to Marcion's threat by simply pointing this out and dismissing his position as incoherent.

The basis for such an argument, complete with an alternative explanation of the world's evil, was available in a theologian in Antioch named Hermogenes. If things had gone differently, Hermogenes might be recognized as the greatest Christian thinker of the period. He was, May points out, "emphatically anxious to ensure the absolute goodness of the creator God." In employing the idea of unoriginate matter, Hermogenes' primary concern was to explain the origin of evil in a way that protected that absolute goodness.* His basic idea, says May, was that "the ground of the evil present in the world" is "the trace of the original disorder of matter remaining in every

---

*May, *Creatio Ex Nihilo*, 146, 140, 145. Although Hermogenes' own writings are no longer extant—they were probably destroyed after his position came to be considered unorthodox— May has reconstructed the main points of his position from the writings of his opponents (see Waszink, *Tertullian: The Treatise against Hermogenes*).

created thing." If, by contrast, we supposed God to have created our world out of nothing, Hermogenes argued, we could have no coherent explanation, "because as perfect Goodness [i.e., God] could only have created good, so the origin of evil would not be explained." The idea of *creatio ex nihilo*, Hermogenes warned his fellow Christian thinkers, would threaten the perfect goodness of God by implying that God is the source of literally everything, including evil.[25]

Besides showing that the doctrine of creation out of chaos protected the absolute goodness of the Creator, Hermogenes argued that it was otherwise perfectly acceptable from the perspective of Christian faith. His contention that Genesis 1:2 supported creation out of chaos followed, May points out, "a widespread expository tradition." Also, far from regarding matter itself as evil, Hermogenes pointed out that "matter before its ordering is without qualities" and therefore "neither good nor evil." Finally, Hermogenes argued, the idea that uncreated matter is coeternal with God does not imply equality. "Hermogenes emphatically declared," says May, "that matter cannot be a principle of equal rank ontologically with God. God is Lord over matter."[26]

However, in spite of the reasonableness of Hermogenes' argument, including his warning that the acceptance of the novel idea of creation out of nothing would give Christians an insoluble problem of evil, Marcion's gnosticism had created such an intense reaction against Platonism that Hermogenes' position did not have a chance. As May says,

In the last decades of the second century the process by which the Catholic Church fenced itself off from the gnostic heretics was in full swing, and with it there was a critical reaction against philosophical reinterpretations of Christian doctrine and especially against all forms of intellectual syncretism. In this historical situation a synthesis of Christianity and Platonism, such as Hermogenes was attempting, could no longer be pursued; to undertake it was, in the atmosphere of anti-gnostic theology, immediately to incur the verdict of heresy.[27]

Accordingly, says May, "When Hermogenes put forward his ideas, literary polemic against him seems to have begun almost immediately."[28]

This polemic against Hermogenes was accompanied by the endorsement of the idea of creation out of absolute nothingness. Hermogenes' earliest opponent, Theophilus of Antioch, was the first Catholic theologian "to use unambiguously the substance and the terminology of the doctrine of *creatio ex nihilo*."* Theophilus's polemical writings influenced Hippolytus, Tertullian, and probably Irenaeus, considered by May the other founder, along with Theophilus himself, "of the church doctrine of *creatio ex nihilo*."[29] The adoption of this novel doctrine occurred with amazing rapidity. The teaching of a thousand years, by the Hebrews and then by the first Christians, was reversed in a generation: "For Tertullian and Hippolytus [and Origen]," says May, "it is already the fixed Christian position that God created the world out of absolutely nothing."[30]

Many decisions made hastily, in a state of mind animated by fury against a heretical movement that seems to threaten one's very existence, are not well thought out—think of the legislation passed in America during the Red Scare of 1919, the McCarthy era, and the current War on Terrorism. There is reason to believe that the same was true of the decision in favor of *creatio ex nihilo*. The rejection of the Platonic idea that our world was created out of unformed matter was based entirely on guilt by association. Because Marcion's idea that this matter could be evil was incoherent, his theology could have been defeated by ridicule, at least by theologians with Hermogenes' philosophical acumen.

However, even though May himself believes that the direction taken by Hermogenes' opponents was the right one, he makes several comments that suggest that they were not intellectually equipped to be carrying out such a momentous change. For example, May points out that the doctrine of *creatio ex nihilo*, which "removes all restrictions on God's creative activity by declaring the free decision of God's will [to be] the sole ground of creation," was bound to make the biblical concept of God "a philosophical problem." May then

---

*Ibid., 147. May uses the term "unambiguously" here to contrast Theophilus's position with the earlier position of Justin's pupil Tatian, in writings evidently directed against Marcion. Suggesting the two-stage theory of creation, Tatian said that God produced matter, but he did not employ the language of *creatio ex nihilo* (ibid., 150–54).

says, "But this is a question far beyond Theophilus." "Theophilus did not," May adds, "fully realize what a radical break with the theological tradition the doctrine of *creatio ex nihilo* constituted."[31]

With regard to Irenaeus, May praises his rejection of the Platonic view that God can will only "the best possible." And May approves his endorsement of "the absolute freedom and omnipotence of the biblical God," which "must rule and dominate in everything" so that "everything else must give way to it."[32] But May then says, "Beyond the demands of the controversy with gnosticism, cosmological questions scarcely worried Irenaeus. For him, it was enough to know that God has produced matter; about the 'How' of its creation [he did not speculate]."[33] Adding that "Irenaeus did not discuss the problems of creation on the philosophical level of his time," May even makes the astonishingly damning statement that his position was "only attainable because Irenaeus is quite unaware of philosophical problems."[34] It is important to remember that May, in speaking of the philosophical limitations of Theophilus and Irenaeus, is speaking about the two theologians most responsible for the fact that the doctrine of *creatio ex nihilo* became the orthodox position within the Christian tradition.

The move to the doctrine of creation out of absolute nothingness turned out to be the most fateful decision made in the history of Christian theology. Spearheaded by theologians who were uninterested in taking a circumspect view of things because of their single-minded focus on the threat to Christian faith from Marcion's gnosticism, and who evidently were also intellectually unequipped to do so, this adoption of *creatio ex nihilo* was made without due regard to the warning by Hermogenes about the threat to Christian faith implicit in *this* doctrine—the threat to the perfect goodness of God. The history of the discussion of the problem of evil would bear out his warning that if God is said to have created the world out of absolute nothingness, the origin of evil cannot be explained, at least without implying that God's goodness is less than perfect. This problem would become one of the major reasons for the rejection of theism in modern times. The doctrine of *creatio ex nihilo* also produced, or at least exacerbated, other problems. I will first discuss the problem of evil, then mention some of the other problems.

4. *Creatio ex Nihilo* and the Problem of Evil

Christian faith might have had a serious problem of evil, even if the doctrine of *creatio ex nihilo* had not been accepted. For one thing, there are statements in both testaments suggesting divine omnipotence. Genesis 18:14, for example, asks rhetorically, "Is anything too hard for the Lord?" And Matthew 19:26 declares, "With God all things are possible." These passages were emphasized, furthermore, by some early Christian theologians who affirmed the Platonic view of creation out of chaos. For example, although Justin Martyr said that "God in his godness created everything from formless matter," he also said that "[o]ne must not doubt that God can do anything that he wills." Justin regarded the incarnation and resurrection to be possible, May points out, because of "the omnipotence of God, to whom the impossible is possible."[35] This kind of thinking might have become normative, in any case, so there is a possibility that Christianity might have had a serious problem of evil even without the doctrine of *creatio ex nihilo*.

Nonetheless, the acceptance of this doctrine was crucial, because it turned this possibility into an inevitability. It also made the resulting problem even more severe. Apart from the doctrine of *creatio ex nihilo*, the biblical passages suggesting absolute omnipotence could have been interpreted in light of other passages, which are legion, suggesting that God cannot simply bring about whatever God wills to happen. The strand in the Hebrew Bible suggesting divine omnipotence might have been interpreted in light of the strand, to which Levenson calls attention, that stresses the continuing power of chaos to thwart divine purposes. The adoption of the doctrine of *creatio ex nihilo*, however, precluded this possibility, with the result that subsequent Christian theologians were given the task of solving an insoluble problem of evil—without, of course, being given their God's power to do the impossible.

This task, solving the problem of evil, has come to be called *theodicy*, which means "justifying the ways of God"—in other words, showing that the creator of this world is good, in spite of the world's evils. Traditional theodicy—meaning theodicy carried out in terms of the traditional idea of divine omnipotence, based on the doctrine of *creatio ex nihilo*—has taken two major forms, depending on whether or not God is said to determine *all* events in the world. The doctrine that God does so can be called "traditional all-determining theism." Because it emerged first, being dominant at least until the eighteenth century, I will examine it first.

The Theodicy of Traditional All-Determining Theism

The most important theologian in the early centuries to take up the task of defending the divine goodness was Augustine. He had for a time been a member of the Manichean movement, which resolved the problem of evil in the same way as Marcion did, that is, by regarding this world as inherently evil. After becoming a Christian, Augustine rejected this view, arguing that everything in this world, having been created *ex nihilo* by an all-good God, is essentially good. The question was whether he could, in light of both Christian doctrine and the world's evils, defend the complete goodness of God.

With regard to Christian doctrine, Augustine recognized that an apparent problem arises from the twofold fact that evidently a majority of the human race is to be condemned to eternal punishment and that the question of who is saved is decided solely by God.[36] Augustine's answer to this apparent problem is that *all* people deserve hell, because they have all freely sinned, so we should praise God for graciously deciding to save some of us.[37] Augustine's defense, as this answer shows, depends on the reality of human freedom. Humans must have the power of free choice, he pointed out, or the whole notion of moral commands would be nonsensical; and if sin were not voluntary, it would not be sin.[38] Human beings must exert volition that does not come from God, he added, or else God would be the author of sin![39]

Although this all makes good sense, Augustine's position on divine omnipotence makes the existence of genuine human freedom inconceivable. "Nothing," he says, "happens unless the Omnipotent wills it to happen. He either allows it to happen or he actually causes it to happen."[40] This statement about "allowing" things to happen might seem to leave room for freedom, but other statements rule out this possibility. Although Augustine had said that there is one thing in the world that was not created by God—namely, the evil will—he insists that all wills, including evil ones, are *ruled* by God.[41] Those wills "which follow the world," he says, "are so entirely at the disposal of God, that He turns them whithersoever He wills, and whensoever He wills." God "does in the hearts of even wicked men whatsoever He wills."[42] The fact that human beings and wicked angels sin, Augustine insists, does not mean that creaturely wills have ever prevented God from accomplishing what God willed.[43] "For who will dare to believe or say," Augustine asks rhetorically, "that it was not in God's power to prevent both angels and men from sinning?"[44]

This position creates a problem of understanding how human sin is possible. Augustine had defined human sin as human beings doing what they will, not what God has willed.[45] But if our wills are completely controlled by God, how can we sin? Augustine tries to solve this problem by distinguishing between two divine wills: the eternal will and the commanding will. When we say that our will, even when we sin, is controlled by God's will, we are speaking of God's eternal will, by which all things are brought about. When we say that sin goes against God's will, we are referring to God's commanding will—what God through Scripture has told us to do and not to do.

This answer, however, still seems to leave an enormous problem. If our sinful choices are themselves fully determined by God's eternal will, how can we be held responsible for them? Augustine himself had said that if sin is not voluntary, it is not sin. His answer to this question involves the position known as *compatibilism*, according to which the fact that our decisions are determined, so that we could not have decided otherwise, does not prevent our decisions from being free. Augustine says, for example, that faith and works are both commanded and said to be God's gifts so that "we may understand both that we do them, and that God makes us to do them."[46] Augustine's entire defense of God's goodness, therefore, hangs by the thread of compatibilism, according to which we can justly be punished for actions, even though we could not have done otherwise—and even though we were caused to do the actions by the punisher.

This issue was discussed more fully by Thomas Aquinas, who also emphasized human freedom in his attempt to defend the goodness of

God. Thomas, as we saw in the previous chapter, employed the scheme of primary and secondary causation. According to this scheme, Thomas emphasized, an event is not done partly by God and partly by the secondary cause, but wholly by God and wholly by the secondary cause.[47] Thomas concedes that it is difficult to understand why, if God wholly brings about all events, the secondary causes are not superfluous. But, he maintains nonetheless, the secondary causes are really causes: "The causality of the lower type of effects is not to be attributed to divine power in such a way as to take away the causality of lower agents."[48] God has, Thomas says, imparted the dignity of causality to creatures in general, and the dignity of free will to human beings in particular.[49] The world's evil is attributable not to God but to defective secondary causes.[50] But how can this be, if God, as the primary cause of all events, is wholly, not merely partly, responsible for them? Thomas himself says that the secondary causes execute God's orders, and that God's will, which is always fulfilled, cannot be hindered by a defect in a secondary cause.[51] With regard to our acts of free choice in particular, Thomas says that God causes them. What could one conclude, other than that the free will of which Thomas speaks is an illusion?

This conclusion was, in fact, reached and explicitly stated by Martin Luther, most clearly in *On the Bondage of the Will*. Rejecting the claim of theologians who say that God's foreknowledge does not prevent human decisions from being free, Luther announced that he had a "bombshell" that "knocks 'free-will' flat." This bombshell was "that God foreknows nothing contingently, but that He foresees, purposes, and does all things according to His own immutable, eternal, and infallible will." Therefore, "all we do, however it may appear to us to be done mutably and contingently, is in reality done necessarily."[52] Since "nothing happens but at [God's] will," Luther adds, "there can be no 'free-will' in man, or angel, or in any creature."[53] Even though some Luther scholars have claimed that Luther means to deny freedom only in relation to salvation and not in respect to human decisions regarding, say, money, Luther says even "that very 'free-will' is overruled by the free-will of God."[54] Leaving no doubt, Luther says that "'free-will' is obviously a term applicable only to the Divine Majesty. . . . If 'free will' is ascribed to men, it is ascribed with no more propriety than divinity itself would be—and no blasphemy could exceed that!"[55]

If Luther, unlike Augustine and Aquinas, does not even make a pretense of ascribing freedom to us, then how can we consider God to be good? Luther acknowledges that this is a problem:

> You may be worried that it is hard to defend the mercy and equity of God in damning the undeserving, that is, ungodly persons, who, being born in ungodliness, can by no means avoid being ungodly, and staying so, and being damned, but are compelled by natural necessity to sin and perish.[56]

Luther agrees that God does seem unjust, but Christian faith, he says, involves "believing Him just when to us He seems unjust."[57]

> This is the highest degree of faith, to believe him merciful when he saves so few and damns so many, and to believe him righteous when by his own will he makes us necessarily damnable, so that he seems . . . to delight in the torments of the wretched and to be worthy of hatred rather than of love.[58]

We are tempted to ask, Luther acknowledges, why God caused Adam to fall, why God created us with Adam's taint of sin when God could have created us out of other material, or why God punishes people for sin they cannot avoid. Luther's answer is that it is not "lawful" to ask such questions. "It is not for us to inquire into these mysteries, but to adore them."[59]

Luther's ultimate answer to all these questions involves his extreme voluntarism, according to which there is nothing prior to, or higher than, the will of God. In Luther's words:

> God is He for Whose will no cause or ground may be laid down as its rule and standard; for nothing is on a level with it or above it, but it is itself the rule for all things. . . . What God wills is not right because He ought . . . so to will; on the contrary, what takes place must be right, because He so wills it.[60]

We see here one of the ultimate implications of the doctrine of *creatio ex nihilo*. Everything was created by God's will, even the standards of good and evil, so whatever God wills is by definition good. Might—at least in the case of the Almighty—makes right.

John Calvin's position is essentially the same. God is called omnipotent, Calvin says in his *Institutes of the Christian Religion*, not because of an ability that sometimes sits idle, but because God determines all things, including "the plans and intentions of men."[61] Against Thomists, who spoke as if God merely permitted evil, Calvin says, "They babble and talk absurdly who, in place of God's Providence, substitute bare permission—as if God sat in a watchtower awaiting chance events."[62] With regard to how humans can sin if all their desires and actions are determined by God, Calvin employs the distinction between God's hidden will, which causes the acts, and God's commanding will, which the actions violate.[63] Although sinners could not have acted otherwise, they are condemned by God because "God does not inquire into what men have been able to do . . . but what they have willed to do."[64] In other words, God condemns people because they have willed to do evil; God ignores the fact that it was the divine will itself that caused them to will evil.

Calvin is perhaps most famous, or notorious, for explicitly affirming double predestination. It is childish, Calvin held, to try to say that God elects only some but does not condemn the rest. "Those whom God passes over, he condemns; and this he does for no other reason than that he wills to exclude them from the inheritance."[65] Referring to the fact that the divine decree predestined so many people, including infants, to eternal death simply because it so pleased God, Calvin says, "The decree is dreadful indeed, I confess."[66] But we are in no position to judge God, he says, exemplifying his extreme voluntarism. "God's will is so much the highest rule of righteousness that whatever he wills, by the very fact that he wills it, must be considered righteous."[67]

However, Calvin, like the other all-determining theists, does not base his defense entirely on this notion that whatever God does is righteous by definition. The final outcome of the world, he also says, will show "that God always has the best reason for his plan."[68] In saying this, he was echoing Luther, who said that at the end of time God will be revealed "as a God Whose justice is most righteous and evident."[69] Luther's position, that evil will finally be seen to be illusory, was in turn essentially the same as that of Thomas, who argued that the evils of which we complain, from a partial viewpoint, actually contribute to the perfection of the whole, so they are not really evil.* This aesthetic analogy had been employed earlier by Augustine, who said that "even what is called evil . . . commends the good . . . , since good things yield greater pleasure and praise when compared to the bad things."[70] Accordingly, says Thomas, just as a good poem or painting is made more beautiful by contrasts, "the universe is beautified even by sinners."[71] This position, that none of the world's apparent evil is genuinely evil, was summed up in the claim by Gottfried Wilhelm Leibniz, at the outset of the eighteenth century, that our world is "the best of all possible worlds."† This conclusion was, of course, implicit in all-determining theism from the outset. As Augustine said, "If it were not good that evil things exist, they would certainly not be allowed to exist by the Omnipotent Good."[72]

The problem with this position is that the occurrence of a single instance of genuine evil—of something that does not contribute to the greatest possible good—implies that God does not exist. And can anyone really doubt that genuinely bad things happen? Could any of us go through the day, reading the newspaper, watching television, and simply facing the trials and tribulations of everyday life, while believing that everything that happens works out for the best? Can any of us believe that the gassing and burning of children at Auschwitz, and the rape and murder of little girls in America, have not made the world worse than it might have been? In the chapter entitled "Rebellion" in Dostoevsky's *The Brothers Karamazov,* Ivan protests against the idea that anything could turn horrible evil into good. Ivan admits that a "higher harmony" may be realized at the end of the world, and that if he is there he may join in the chorus shouting, "Thou art just, O Lord, for Thy ways are revealed." He says, however, that he wants to give his ticket back in advance, because he hopes he would never accept the idea that the suffering of innocent children was necessary for some higher good. The conviction that

---

*"Since God," says Thomas, "provides universally for all being, it belongs to His providence to permit certain defects in particular effects, that the perfect good of the universe may not be hindered, for if all evil were prevented much good would be absent from the universe" (*Summa Theologica*, 1. 22.2, ad 3).

†Leibniz used this phrase in his *Theodicy*, which was the first book with this title. I discuss Leibniz's position in my *God, Power, and Evil*, chap. 11.

evils of this world are not canceled out from some higher perspective is also voiced by Alfred North Whitehead, who says, "The Leibnizian theory of the 'best of possible worlds' is an audacious fudge produced in order to save the face of a Creator constructed by contemporary, and antecedent, theologians."[73]

Luther, one of those antecedent theologians, sought to make this theory credible by distinguishing between three lights: those of nature, grace, and glory. God governs the world in such a way, Luther says, that according to the light of nature, or natural reason, one would conclude either that there is no God, or that God is unjust, because the wicked prosper and the good suffer. But this problem, he says, is cleared up by the light of grace, which teaches: *"There is a life after this life; and all that is not punished and repaid here will be punished and repaid there."* In providing this answer, Luther admits, the light of grace creates a new problem, because "it is inexplicable how God can damn him who by his own strength can do nothing but sin and become guilty," so the fault still seems to lie "in the injustice of God." But, because the light of grace easily solves the problem that was insoluble by the light of nature, Luther says, it is reasonable to assume that "the light of glory will . . . solve problems that are insoluble in the light of . . . grace."[74]

Although this argument may seem plausible at first sight, it is problematic. If we cannot see now, by the light of grace, how the second problem is soluble, then even the first problem has not been solved for us. It has, in fact, been exacerbated, because many of the wicked, far from prospering in this life, have a rather miserable existence. The light of grace, as interpreted by Luther, tells us that they will also be miserable for eternity, even though the fact that they were wicked was due to God's all-determining will.

For this and related reasons, Christian faith, as presented by all-determining theists, not only did not solve the problem of evil but increased it. In addition to the standard questions, this theology added the question of God's justice with regard to salvation and damnation. Especially troubling was the idea that people have no freedom vis-à-vis God. Besides implying that God was damning them for failings that God had foreordained, this doctrine, many complained, induced fatalism and passivity.

Furthermore, the doctrine that human actions are totally determined by God is, like the closely related belief that nothing truly evil occurs, a belief that no one can consistently live out in practice. For example, Calvin says that meditation on the idea that God causes all things, even the acts of our enemies, helps us develop "patience in adversity." The most "effective remedy for anger and impatience," says Calvin, is to remember with regard to any event that "the Lord has willed it" and that "he wills nothing but what is just and expedient." Accordingly, "when we are unjustly wounded by men, let us . . . remember . . . that whatever our enemy has wickedly committed against us was permitted and sent by God's just dispensation."[75] But when Calvin is doing battle with his intellectual opponents, we see that he does not really believe this. For example, he describes people who reject the doctrine of double predestination as "dogs [who] assail this doctrine with their venomous bitings," dismissing their objections as the "petulance [of] impious and profane men"[76]—obviously forgetting that, by his doctrine, they are as fully caused by God to raise these objections as Calvin is to teach what he does. He remembers his doctrine, to be sure, when he is defending his own teaching. Believing that it has been produced by the Holy Spirit, he says that his opponents merely pretend that their complaints are directed at him because they do not dare openly "to vomit forth these blasphemies against heaven."[77] But, given Calvin's belief that God causes these people to criticize his doctrine, is he not here implicitly accusing God of blasphemy? Calvin himself opens the door to this question. Against those who fear to teach double predestination openly because it might induce fatalism and passivity, Calvin says that such people "accuse God indirectly of stupid thoughtlessness, as if he had not foreseen the peril that they feel they have wisely met."[78] Analogously, when Calvin accuses his opponents of teaching false and harmful doctrines, is he not indirectly accusing God, who caused those opponents to say what they did, of having produced false and harmful teaching? As these illustrations show, even Calvin, meditate as he might on the idea that divine providence totally determines all things, could not really believe that we do not act with a degree of freedom.

For these and related reasons, some philosophers and theologians, while still accepting the doctrine of *creatio ex nihilo*, began reconceiving the relation of God to the world to make room for human freedom. This doctrine can, accordingly, be called "traditional free will theism." This name distinguishes this position from that of Augustine and Thomas because, although those theologians verbally affirmed human freedom, their system, as Luther and Calvin pointed out, actually had no room for it, because they maintained that all things are determined by God.

The Theodicy of Traditional Free Will Theism

Traditional free will theists, still accepting the doctrine of *creatio ex nihilo*, hold that God *could* determine all things. But, they say, God has voluntarily, through a self-limitation on the divine power, given real freedom to at least some of the creatures, especially humans. Real freedom means that their decisions and actions are not fully determined by God; these theists reject the sophism that human freedom is compatible with complete divine determination. This allowance for human self-determination, these theists point out, means that we can do justice to our inevitable presupposition that human beings are partly free, and hence partly responsible, for their actions. We can also, therefore, speak meaningfully of human sin, of actions that go contrary to the divine will, without resorting to the sophism of two divine wills. It would seem, therefore, that this version of traditional theism is in position to develop a better theodicy. And it is. But it also retains some severe problems.*

One problem follows from the fact that traditional free will theists usually regard human beings as the only creatures on this planet with freedom. It thereby provides no answer to the problem of what is usually called "natural evil," meaning the forms of evil that are not due to human volition, such as earthquakes, tornadoes, hurricanes, droughts, floods, and disease. This problem was central to the transi-

---

*I have provided extensive criticisms of traditional free will theism (alternatively called "hybrid" and "classical" free will theism) in *God, Power, and Evil*, chap. 13 (on John Hick's theodicy); *Evil Revisited*, chaps. 1, 5; my contributions to Davis, ed., *Encountering Evil*; and in "Process Theology and the Christian Good News: A Response to Classical Free Will Theism," "In Response to William Hasker," "Traditional Free Will Theodicy and Process Theodicy: Hasker's Claim for Parity," and "On Hasker's Attempt to Defend His Parity Claim."

tion from deism to atheism in eighteenth-century France. Voltaire, the famous French deist who ridiculed the idea that the Bible was written by God, parodied in his *Candide* the view that this world, with all of its historical details, is "the best of all possible worlds." Voltaire, like other deists, advocated a religion based not on history but solely on nature. The order and design of nature, he believed, pointed to the existence of a good creator who sanctioned a religion oriented around morality. However, the terrible Lisbon earthquake of 1755, in which thousands of innocents were killed, shook this belief, leading Voltaire, in his *Poem on the Lisbon Disaster*, to doubt that deism could provide any better explanation for evil than could orthodox Christianity.* In Hume's *Dialogues concerning Natural Religion*, furthermore, the position of Cleanthes, the deist, is rejected as firmly as that of Demea, the traditional theist, with the problem of natural evil playing a central role in the argument.

A second problem with traditional free will theism is that according to its hypothesis, God could intervene to prevent any specific instance of evil. God could have diverted every bullet headed toward a human being "too young to die." God could have prevented any of the massacres that have occurred. God could, in fact, prevent any sinful human intention from producing its intended effects. And God could prevent any disease or any natural disaster from producing permanent injury, agonizing suffering, or premature death. This position, therefore, retains the assumption of traditional theism that has led millions to question the existence or at least the goodness of God. If there were a Superman who could prevent all these kinds of events but refused to do so—perhaps on the grounds that we will be taught patience by having to endure these sufferings—we would certainly question his moral goodness. A Superman, of course, could not prevent all genuine evils, because, being finite, he could not be everywhere at once. But the God of traditional theism, being ubiquitous, does not have this excuse. Such reflections led Stendhal to make his famous quip: "God's only excuse is that he does not exist."†

---

*This earthquake, which produced tidal floods and raging fires, is compared with the terrorist attacks of September 11, 2001, by Susan Neiman in *Evil in Modern Thought*.

†"Stendhal" was the pen name of the French biographer and historian Marie Henri Beyle (1783–1842).

Some traditional free will theists, facing such problems, simply say that although they cannot explain why God allows so much evil, they need not do so. "If God is good and powerful as the theist believes," says Alvin Plantinga, "then he will indeed have a good reason for permitting evil; but why suppose the theist must be in a position to figure out what it is?"[79] Plantinga's answer here is part of his claim that theists need not offer a *theodicy*, which would attempt to provide a plausible explanation for the world's evils, but can rest content with a *defense*, which merely shows that there is no logical contradiction between holding that "evil exists" and that "God is omnipotent, omniscient, and wholly good." As long as an explanation shows how these two propositions *might* be consistent, says Plantinga, the fact that it is implausible "is utterly beside the point."[80] To many critics, however, this kind of "defense" is an admission, in effect, that traditional theism, even in its free will form, cannot be made plausible.

5. Other Distortions Due to *Creatio ex Nihilo*

The doctrine of *creatio ex nihilo* led the Christian "good news" to come to seem like bad news, like such a horrible view of the universe that Voltaire's battle cry against Christianity was "crush the infamous thing."* One of the greatest distortions of Christian faith is surely the fact that it came to be equated with such a horrible worldview. There are, however, still other distortions that were created, or at least exacerbated, by the doctrine of *creatio ex nihilo*.

A closely related, equally enormous distortion, which contributed to the widespread conviction among progressive thinkers that Christianity needed to be crushed, was the fact that it had come to be identified with the social, political, and economic status quo. As we saw, the desire to undergird the established order against radicals, who endorsed such revolutionary ideas as democracy and economic justice, was one of the major motives of those who adopted the mechan-

---

*Franklin Baumer uses this phrase as the title for the chapter on the eighteenth century in his *Religion and the Rise of Scepticism.*

ical view of nature to support the immortality of the soul and the existence of a supernatural deity. The most famous critique of Christianity from this standpoint was, of course, that of Karl Marx. His criticism of religion as the "opiate of the people" referred precisely to the idea that religion, by which he primarily meant Christianity, conditions people to accept injustice by teaching them that the present order is divinely ordained and that the sufferings of this world are unimportant in comparison with the glory of the world to come—when we will see, as Luther said, that everything had been as it ought to have been. Through the influence of Marx, hundreds of millions of people have been taught that Christianity is necessarily hostile to concern for social justice for the poor and disenfranchised. Given the fact that Jesus' own message focused heavily on social and economic justice for the poor and disenfranchised of his time, and that he was crucified by the political establishment with the aid of a corrupt religious establishment,[81] a greater distortion of Christian faith is hard to imagine.

Another distortion related to the doctrine of *creatio ex nihilo* has involved the desire to prove Christianity to be the "one true religion." For example, Tertullian, regarding the bodily resurrection of Jesus as *the* miracle that put the divine stamp of approval on Christianity, used the doctrine of *creatio ex nihilo* as proof that God had the power to awaken the dead.[82] This doctrine was also used to support the church's supernaturalistic Christology, according to which God's presence in Jesus was different in kind from God's presence in the Hebrew prophets and Mohammed—a doctrine that was not irrelevant to the Crusades. This supernaturalistic Christology, according to which Jesus was God, also lay behind the charge that Jews were guilty of "deicide"—a charge central to the horrible history of defamation and persecution that eventuated in the Holocaust. Also, one of the main motives for rejecting magical naturalism in favor of the mechanistic view of nature was, as we saw in the previous chapter, the desire by Christians such as Mersenne and Boyle to continue arguing that the miracles proved Christianity to be the one true religion.

Another type of distortion resulted from the fact, discussed in the previous chapter, that the strategy of the seventeenth-century founders of modern science, insofar as they intended to support a supernaturalistic version of Christian faith, backfired. "The scientific worldview" soon came to be equated with an atheistic, materialistic version of naturalism. Modern liberal theology, not wanting to be in opposition to science, has attempted, in various ways, to reinterpret Christian faith so that it is compatible with this worldview. These attempts have resulted in formulations of the content of Christian faith that are distorted, not by being horrible, but by being largely vacuous, unable to support vital Christian communities. I will deal with this problem in the following chapters.

For now I close by repeating the thesis of the present chapter—that Christian faith is a great truth, but one that has been grossly distorted. In my final two chapters, I will suggest how we can, while recognizing the great truth in scientific naturalism, reformulate Christian faith so as to make its great truth manifest. In doing so, I will be employing and explaining the position known as "process theology," which is based on the process philosophy developed by Alfred North Whitehead and Charles Hartshorne.

NOTES

1. See Niebuhr, "As Deceivers Yet True"; and "The Truth in Myths."

2. See Schmookler, *The Parable of the Tribes*; Lerner, *The Creation of Patriarchy*; and Suchocki, *The Fall to Violence*.

3. I have developed this notion of the demonic in a set of published lectures entitled "Postmodern Theology for the Church," especially the lectures entitled "Why Demonic Power Exists: Understanding the Church's Enemy" and "Overcoming the Demonic: The Church's Mission." See also "Divine Goodness and Demonic Evil." This idea of the demonic is central to a book in progress about American imperialism as interpreted from the perspective of Christian faith.

4. Levenson, *Creation and the Persistence of Evil*, 121.

5. Ibid., 5, 121.

6. Ibid., 121, 157 n 12.

7. Ibid., 4, 123.

8. Plato, *Timaeus* 30A.

9. Erickson, *Christian Theology*, 374.

10. Levenson, *Creation and the Persistence of Evil*, xiii, 49, 50.

11. Ibid., 7–18.

12. Ibid., xiii.

13. Ibid., 12, 26, 122–23.

14. May, *Creatio Ex Nihilo: The Doctrine of "Creation out of Nothing" in Early Christian Thought*, xi–xii, 7.

15. Ibid., 7–8, 11, 16.

16. Ibid., 21.

17. Ibid., xi.

18. Ibid., 27.

19. Ibid., 3–4.

20. Ibid., 27.

21. Ibid., 122. See also Barnard, *Justin Martyr*, 111–13.

22. Ibid., xiii, 24.

23. Ibid., 40, 56.

24. Ibid., 56 n, 152.

25. Ibid., 142, 141.

26. Ibid., 144, 142, 141.

27. Ibid., 146.

28. Ibid., 140. See also Waszink, *Tertullian: The Treatise against Hermogenes*.

29. Ibid., 147, 159, 178.

30. Ibid., 178.

31. Ibid., 161, 163.

32. Ibid., 167–68, 174.

33. Ibid., 173–74.

34. Ibid., 174, 177.

35. Ibid., 122, 129.

36. Augustine, *City of God*, trans. Marcus Dods, 21.12; *Enchiridion*, trans. J. F. Shaw, 24.97; *Grace and Free Will*, trans. P. Holmes, 45; *On the Predestination of the Saints*, trans. R. E. Wallis, 11, 19, 34 (all in Oates, ed., *Basic Writings of St. Augustine*).

37. Augustine, *City of God*, 12.8; *Enchiridion*, 25.99; *Predestination*, 16.

38. Augustine, *Grace and Free Will*, 2, 4; *Of True Religion*, trans. John H. S. Burleigh, 14.27 (in *Augustine: Earlier Writings*).

39. Augustine, *On the Spirit and the Letter*, trans. P. Holmes, 54 (in Oates, ed., *Basic Writings of St. Augustine*).

40. Augustine, *Enchiridion*, 24.95.

41. Augustine, *City of God*, 5.8, 10; 11.17.

42. Augustine, *Grace and Free Will*, 41, 42.

43. Augustine, *Enchiridion*, 24.95.

44. Augustine, *City of God*, 4.27.

45. Augustine, *Enchiridion*, 26.100.

46. Augustine, *Predestination,* 22.

47. Thomas Aquinas, *Summa Contra Gentiles*, 3.1.70.8.

48. Ibid., 3.1.69.

49. Thomas Aquinas, *Summa Theologica*, 1.23.3, ad 2, 3; 1.22.3, ans.

50. Thomas Aquinas, *Summa Contra Gentiles*, 3.1.10.7; 3.1.71.2 and 13; *Summa Theologica*, 1.49.2.

51. Thomas Aquinas, *Summa Theologica*, 1.22.3, ad 3; 1.19.6, ans and ad 3; 1.19.8, ans.

52. Luther, *On the Bondage of the Will*, 614–20. (The numbers refer to the lines of the Weimar edition of Luther's works, which are given in the translation used here.)

53. Ibid., 784–86.

54. Ibid., 634–39.

55. Ibid., 104–7.

56. Ibid., 784–86.

57. Ibid.

58. Ibid., 632–33.

59. Ibid., 684–86, 711–14.

60. Ibid., 711–14.

61. Calvin, *Institutes of the Christian Religion*, 1.16.3; 1.16.8.

62. Ibid., 1.18.1.

63. Ibid., 1.18.3.

64. Ibid., 1.18.4.

65. Ibid., 3.23.1.

66. Ibid., 3.23.7.

67. Ibid., 3.23.2.

68. Ibid., 1.17.1.

69. Luther, *On the Bondage of the Will*, 784–86.

70. Augustine, *Enchiridion*, 3.11.

71. Thomas Aquinas, *Summa Contra Gentiles*, 11.23.

72. Augustine, *Enchiridion*, 24.96.

73. Whitehead, *Process and Reality*, 47.

74. Luther, *On the Bondage of the Will*, 784–86.

75. Calvin, *Institutes*, 1.17.8.

76. Ibid., 1.17.2; 1.18.3.

77. Ibid., 1.17.2.

78. Ibid., 3.21.5.

79. Plantinga, "Reply to the Basingers on Divine Omnipotence," 28.

80. Ibid.

81. See Horsley, *Jesus and the Spiral of Violence;* Horsley, *Jesus and Empire;* Sanders, *Jesus and Judaism*; and Fredriksen, *From Jesus to Christ.*

82. See May, *Creatio Ex Nihilo*, 137. For another recent work in theological reconstruction that has employed May's book in rejecting the doctrine of *creation ex nihilo,* see Catherine Keller, *The Face of the Deep.*

Chapter 3

Scientific Naturalism and Christian Faith

A New Synthesis

*I*n the previous chapters, I have described seven attempts to synthesize Christian faith and the naturalism that emerged in the Greek tradition. In the first of these, which involved Christian faith prior to the rise of the doctrine of *creatio ex nihilo*, there was at least the possibility that a real synthesis might have emerged. The primary doctrines of the Christian faith and the naturalism of the Greek tradition might have been equally endorsed, without compromising either one. In the subsequent syntheses, either one tradition or the other was compromised. In the syntheses created by Irenaeus and Augustine, by Thomas Aquinas, by the Reformers and their voluntarist forerunners, and by the early modern thinkers, the naturalism of the Greek tradition was compromised in the name of the absolute freedom and omnipotence of God implied by the doctrine of *creatio ex nihilo*. In the deistic synthesis, both sides were compromised, as *creatio ex nihilo* was retained and yet ongoing divine activity in the world and human experience of God were not allowed. In the late modern synthesis, nothing is left of Christian faith except for a linguistic shadow of the voluntarist idea of God as reflected in the legal-mechanical view of the early modern thinkers—the reference to the world's regularities as the "laws of nature." The mechanistic view of nature, along with the sensationist doctrine of perception, had become a Frankenstein monster, destroying not only its creator—the extremely supernaturalistic version of Christian faith—but the possibility of any significantly religious view of the world whatsoever.

In this chapter, I will point to the existence of a new synthesis that emerged in the twentieth century, one that involves a worldview equally adequate for the primary doctrines of the Christian faith and the kind of naturalism required by science. Before describing this new synthesis, however, I need to support the contention that the late modern worldview, which I call naturalism$_{sam}$, has not left room for Christian faith. I will do this by discussing modern liberal theology, which is the movement that tried to accommodate Christian faith to the worldview of the scientific community during the deistic and late modern periods.

1. Modern *Liberal* Theology

In referring to this form of theology as both "modern" and "liberal," I am not being redundant. In my vocabulary, these terms, used in relation to types of theology, point to different issues. To speak of "liberal" theology, as distinct from conservative to fundamentalist theologies, is primarily to refer to a *method* of doing theology. Whereas conservative to fundamentalist theologies use the "method of authority" to settle the question as to what is true and false,* liberal theologies reject this method, instead settling questions of truth and falsity on the basis of common experience and reason—that is, by reasoning on the basis of experience that is at least potentially common to all people.

This method does not mean that there is no room for appeal to the authority of Scripture and tradition. This appeal is crucial to the question of what Christian faith is, as in my attempt to state the primary doctrines of the Christian gospel. For liberal theology, however, settling this question does not settle the question of what is true. This distinction is obvious, of course, with reference to other traditions. To discern the primary doctrines of Buddhism or Marxism, for example, we would need to look at Buddhist scriptures and tradition, or at the writings of Marx and later Marxists; but after deciding what the primary doctrines are, we would still need to ask whether there is good

---

*For a superb discussion of the method of authority, see Farley and Hodgson, "Scripture and Tradition."

reason to think them true. We would use reasoning on the basis of common human experience to answer this question. Liberal theologians say that this distinction between "what is Christian" and "what is true" must also be made with regard to Christian faith, with the latter question settled on the basis of reason and experience.

The basis for this distinction, and hence the liberal method, arises from the rejection of what we can call "epistemic supernaturalism." The word "epistemic" comes from the Greek word *episteme*, which means "understanding" or "knowledge." Epistemic supernaturalism, therefore, refers to the idea that we have some knowledge that has come about supernaturally. Traditionally, in fact, theology was divided into two parts: natural theology and supernatural theology. To speak of natural theology was not to refer to its content, as if it dealt only with nature, meaning the physical world, but to refer to its method—the fact that it dealt only with those things, including things about God, that could be known by relying solely on common human experience and reason, without the aid of special revelation. The heavy use of Aristotle's philosophy in the late Middle Ages was based on the assumption that it was the height of natural knowledge. Supernatural theology, by contrast, was theology based on the special revelation given to Christians, the truth of which was taken to be supernaturally guaranteed by means of infallible revelation and inerrant inspiration. Within that framework, there was no distinction between what is Christian and what is true; to settle the question of what the Christian position is on some issue was simultaneously to settle the question of what the truth is. Liberal theology rejects that equation because it rejects epistemic supernaturalism and thereby the whole basis for speaking of "supernatural theology." The defining characteristic of liberal theology, therefore, is its rejection of the method of authority in favor of epistemic naturalism.

To say that the main thing that distinguishes liberal theology from traditional theology (including what we today call conservative to fundamentalist theologies) is its method is not, however, to deny that this methodological difference is rooted in a difference with regard to the nature of reality. Epistemic supernaturalism, which liberal theology rejects, presupposes supernaturalism in the usual sense of the term, which I have discussed earlier. Supernaturalism in that usual sense can be called "ontological supernaturalism." The word "ontology," derived from the Latin word *ontos*, refers to the doctrine of being, of what exists. Ontological supernaturalism, accordingly, says that there exists a being that can interrupt the world's normal processes.

The ideas of infallible revelation and inerrant inspiration presuppose that this kind of supernatural interruption has occurred. Why? Because the normal way in which human beings arrive at their beliefs is an extremely fallible process, in which false beliefs can enter in through prejudice, wishful thinking, party spirit, the limited information available at a given time and place, and countless other factors. The belief that the ideas put forth by some particular human beings are infallible and inerrant, guaranteed to be devoid of error, presupposes that in these particular human beings the normal human processes of belief formation, with their fallibility and tendency to error, have been supernaturally overruled, so that pure, unadulterated truth came forth. Liberal theology, therefore, rejects ontological supernaturalism in favor what I have called naturalism$_{ns}$.

Actually, to be more precise, liberal theology does not necessarily presuppose naturalism$_{ns}$, which says that interruptions of the world's normal causal processes are strictly impossible. Liberal theology, in rejecting the method of authority, necessarily rejects only the idea that such interruptions have actually occurred, resulting in some infallible revelation. The early deists, as I pointed out, still presupposed the doctrine of *creatio ex nihilo*, which meant that their worldview allowed for the possibility of supernatural interruptions. But they denied that any such interruptions had actually occurred, at least any that guaranteed the truth of the Scriptures or the creeds produced by the early church councils. And there are many liberal theologians even today who reject epistemic supernaturalism without necessarily holding that supernatural revelation would be impossible; they simply believe that it has not occurred. We can say, therefore, that liberal theology presupposes the rejection of the occurrence of supernatural revelation, with *some* liberal theologians rejecting even its possibility.

In any case, liberal Christian theology, by virtue of its acceptance of epistemic naturalism, is methodologically in harmony with modern science, which likewise bases its claims to truth, at least in principle, on reason and experience. Insofar as liberal theology accepts ontological naturalism, it is also in harmony with the basic worldview of today's scientific community. With regard to method and basic worldview, therefore, a modern liberal theology has already achieved a synthesis of Christian faith and scientific naturalism.

However, as a result of its distinctively modern dimension, modern liberal theology's synthesis has been at the expense of its Christian character. Conservative to fundamentalist critics have been right in saying that modern liberal Christian theology has been more modern than Christian. Much of this criticism, to be sure, has involved complaints about secondary or even tertiary matters, such as the rejection of inerrant inspiration, the virgin birth, and the Trinitarian and christological doctrines associated with the councils of Nicaea and Chalcedon. The real problem, however, is that modern liberal theology, by virtue of its modernism, gave up most of the primary doctrines of the Christian gospel. I turn now to this issue.

2. *Modern* Liberal Theology

Liberal theology, I have said, settles the question of what is true, or at least credible, on the basis of reason and experience. We should, I hold, affirm liberal theology, thus understood. The problem with *modern* liberal theology is that it has accepted the distinctively modern ideas about the nature of the world in general and human experience in particular that I discussed in the previous chapters. Modern liberal theology accepted, that is, the mechanistic idea of nature and the sensationist doctrine of human experience. At the same time that it accepted the liberal commitment to rest its case entirely on experience and reason, therefore, modern liberal theology agreed to employ a very impoverished notion of experience, and thereby a very restrictive notion of what could be accepted as reasonable. This acceptance of these modern ideas led modern liberal theology to deny many primary doctrines of Christian faith. Many of these involve the idea of divine activity.

Divine Activity

Christian faith presupposes divine activity in the world in those primary doctrines that speak of creation, providence, revelation, incarnation, and salvation. The deistic form of liberal theology eliminated all of these categories except the original creation of the world. It thus regarded God as wholly transcendent, in the sense of not being immanent in our world. In reaction to this denial of divine presence in the world, romantic and idealistic theologies in the nineteenth century emphasized divine immanence, but this language, when closely analyzed, involved simply a reaffirmation of the primary-secondary scheme, with all miracles omitted, so that divine activity was functionally identical with natural causation. With the adoption of evolutionary ideas, this identification meant the equation of divine activity with the immanent process that has brought about evolutionary progress in both nature and human history. However, given the rejection of miracles, and thereby of any acts that were "acts of God" in a special sense, the language about divine activity came to seem meaningless.*

In reaction, neo-orthodox theologians and the resulting "biblical theology" movement reaffirmed a transcendent deity who acts in the world. For example, in a book entitled *God Who Acts: Biblical Theology as Recital,* G. Ernest Wright said, "The central message of the Bible is a proclamation of the Divine action."[1] When closely examined, however, the language of divine action turned out to be vacuous, as Langdon Gilkey showed in a famous article called "Cosmology, Ontology, and the Travail of Biblical Language." Although these biblical theologians were reaffirming the biblical language of divine acting and speaking, they continued, like the liberal theologians they criticized, to presuppose an unbroken nexus of natural causes and effects.[2] Accordingly, although their language suggested that they were speaking of certain events as being "mighty acts of God," all they were really saying is that the Hebrews or the early Christians *believed* certain events to be special acts of God. Their language of divine action, therefore, was devoid of meaning.[3]

---

*In this account, I have drawn upon Owen Thomas's excellent introduction in his edited volume *God's Activity in the World,* 1–14.

An example of this problem is provided by Rudolf Bultmann, the most influential New Testament theologian in the middle part of the twentieth century, who was famous for his claim that the New Testament needed to be "demythologized." To speak mythologically, he said, is to assert that God has interrupted the natural nexus of cause and effect, thereby treating God as if God were one (secondary) cause among others.[4] We must regard such language as mythological, Bultmann said, partly because "modern science does not believe that the course of nature can be interrupted . . . by supernatural powers."[5] Not only in scientific work but also in daily life, said Bultmann, we necessarily see worldly events as linked by natural causes and effects, "so there remains no room for God's working."[6] Bultmann insisted, nevertheless, that we could speak meaningfully of divine action, especially of Jesus as God's decisive act.[7] The way we can do this, he said, is to affirm a "paradoxical identity" between divine activity and some worldly event that has evoked faith. In a moment of faith, in other words, a person can regard some event as an act of God while still understanding this event "as a link in the chain of the natural course of events."[8] For example, a parent whose child has been healed of an illness can thank God while recognizing that the healing was due to the medicine provided by the doctor. As this example shows, the only thing special about an event called an "act of God" is the fact that it happened to evoke faith in someone.

As this discussion shows, the inability of modern liberal theologians to speak meaningfully of divine activity has been due in part to the fact that they took over the primary-secondary scheme for thinking of the relation of divine and worldly causation. That scheme was always of questionable meaning. Etienne Gilson, a twentieth-century Thomistic defender of this view, acknowledged that to endorse it, "We must hold firmly to two apparently contradictory truths. God does whatever creatures do; and yet creatures themselves do whatever they do."[9] As Gilkey points out, these two "truths" are not only apparently contradictory, but actually so, and this fact became evident once the idea of occasional miraculous interruptions was given up.[10] At least part of the problem, therefore, is due to retaining this primary-secondary scheme while accepting naturalism$_{ns}$.

This problem was further aggravated by the acceptance of the mechanistic idea of nature and the sensationist doctrine of perception. According to the mechanistic idea of nature, the only conceivable kind of causal relation involves the impact of one bit of matter on another. As we saw, this conception of the physical world, and hence of the human body, rendered unintelligible the idea that the human mind or soul, understood as a nonmaterial agent, could affect the body. This mind-body problem led, by analogy, to the God-world problem of how God, understood as an immaterial agent, could influence a material, clocklike world. This problem was difficult enough within a supernaturalistic framework, being a contributor to the transition to deism. Then when the supernaturalistic idea of deity was completely rejected, the idea of divine influence on the physical world became wholly inconceivable. For example, European theologian Willem Drees, who explicitly endorses a materialistic version of scientific naturalism, says that the only religious views of transcendence that would be compatible with naturalism are those that "do not assume that a transcendent realm shows up *within* the natural world."[11]

By itself, the mechanistic idea of nature would have left open the possibility that God could directly affect *human experience* (understood dualistically as outside nature). So, although theologians would not have been able to affirm physical miracles, such as the parting of the Red Sea or the resurrection of the body, they would have been able to affirm divine revelation, inspiration, incarnation, and a general providential activity in human history. Most of the primary doctrines of the Christian faith could have been affirmed. This path was blocked, however, by the fact that the primary-secondary scheme was reinforced with regard to the divine-human relation by the sensationist doctrine of perception, according to which we cannot be influenced naturally by anything beyond ourselves except by means of our sensory organs.

That doctrine was originally intended, as we saw, to limit the divine influence in the world to events of supernatural intervention. But once supernaturalism was rejected, the retention of the sensationist doctrine of perception meant that there could be no divine influence on human experience whatsoever. This fact is reflected in Bultmann's statement that it is just as mythological to speak of "intervention of supernatural powers in the inner life of the soul" as to speak of such intervention in the course of nature.[12] Another example is provided by Drees, who says that no "spiritual realm distinct from the natural world shows up *within* our natural world, not even in the mental life of humans."[13]

Such doctrines would obviously make it difficult for theologians to provide any account of Jesus as an incarnation of God. Many modern theologians, in fact, limit their christological accounts to statements about the *meaning* of Jesus for Christian faith, ignoring the question of how Jesus was related to God. In terms of the traditional division of Christology into "the person and work of Jesus Christ," in other words, they focus exclusively on the "work," ignoring the question about the "person" (except perhaps for purely historical statements about Jesus).

Accounts that do raise the question of Jesus' relation to God typically deny that the language of divine incarnation can be employed in any straightforward way. In a book entitled *The Metaphor of God Incarnate*, for example, John Hick says that we should understand "the idea of divine incarnation as a metaphorical idea," not an idea to be taken literally or metaphysically.[14] To some extent, Hick is thereby simply rejecting the traditional supernaturalistic Christology, according to which the statement that Jesus was "God incarnate" was an abbreviation of "God the son, second person of the holy Trinity, incarnate."[15] Hick's rejection of the idea of divine incarnation, however, is more sweeping, rejecting *any* literal or metaphysical sense in which we can speak of God as present in Jesus.[16]

In an earlier book, Hick had explained the reason for this more sweeping rejection. In a statement reflecting his acceptance of the late modern view, he said, "It is in principle possible, on the basis of the physical and human sciences, to form a picture of the universe, including man, which is complete and yet involves no reference to God." Our theological picture of the universe, he added, must assume that all the present gaps in our knowledge of the causal web will be filled in, so that there will be no events that can be explained only by reference to divine causation.[17] On this basis, Hick suggests that theological language about special acts of God does not really mean to be offering a causal account of the events in question that differs from a nontheistic account. Rather, theological language arises out of a different *perspective*, in which an event is "experienced as" an act of God. Hick says, for example, that "a miracle is any event that is experienced as a miracle."[18] As in the previous accounts we examined, all the specialness of the event is lodged in the believer's response, and none in the event itself.

The implications of such an approach for Christology have been brought out with special clarity by Maurice Wiles (who prior to his retirement was the Regis Professor of Divinity at Christ Church, Oxford). With regard to events that have been accepted as special revelations of God, Wiles says, "It is the qualitative assessment of them, rather than evidence of anything special about the manner of their occurrence, that is determinative. . . . [T]hey [do not] require to be understood as involving any special form of divine activity in the world."[19] In making this statement, Wiles is, in part, simply ruling out the occasional occurrence of "special supernatural causation."[20] But he goes beyond this rejection of supernatural interventions to make the denial, common to all forms of deism, that there is any variability whatsoever in the divine influence in the world.[21] Wiles, in fact, accepts the deistic label, saying that his position "is deistic in so far as it refrains from claiming any effective causation on the part of God in relation to particular occurrences."[22]

This view creates problems for Christology, Wiles realizes, because the special authority given to Jesus "has normally been understood to involve some kind of special divine action" in him.[23] Not being able to affirm that the divine action in Jesus was in itself special in any way, Wiles says that the most we can say is that Jesus was "more fully responsive to the divine action than others," so that "we might rightly speak of the events of [his life] as acts of God in a special sense towards those of us who are influenced by them."[24] Wiles's account does say that Jesus was special prior to the believers' response to him. But by presupposing a deistic version of the primary-secondary scheme, according to which the only divine causation in the world is God's invariable sustaining activity, Wiles's account cannot explain this specialness, even partly, by speaking of divine action that was special in any sense.

Religious Experience

The reverse side of the impossibility of speaking of divine influence on human experience is the impossibility of affirming genuine religious experience,* understood as a direct experience of God (as distinct from merely *interpreting* the world *as* God's world). Part of the reason for the early modern insistence on the sensationist doctrine of perceptual experience, as we saw, was precisely for the sake of ruling out enthusiasm. Immanuel Kant, one of the most important philosophers of the eighteenth-century Enlightenment, exemplified this connection in his book entitled, significantly, *Religion within the Limits of Reason Alone.* To believe in a "feeling of the immediate presence of the Supreme Being," said Kant, would be a "fanatical religious illusion." Why? Because it would be to affirm "a receptivity for an intuition for which there is no sensory provision in man's nature."[25] Kant's acceptance of the sensationist doctrine of perception is shown by his assumption that we can have no experience ("intuition") of something for which we have no sensory organ. The resulting idea, that there can be no direct experience of God, has become a dogma of modern philosophy. For example, one recent philosopher, J. J. C. Smart, explained why mystical experiences are impossible by saying that "getting in touch" with things, such as rabbits or even electrons, involves responses to physical stimuli, whereas so-called mystical experience would involve getting in touch with something nonphysical. Therefore, Smart concluded, all apparent mystical experience must be illusory.[26]

This denial of the possibility of genuine religious experience has played a major role in the modern study of religion. One of the founders of the sociology of religion, Emile Durkheim, said that the primary problem in understanding religion is "explaining the sacred"—that is, explaining why religious people think in terms of the distinction between the "sacred" and the "profane," even though "nothing in sensible [i.e., sensory] experience seems able to suggest the idea of so radical a duality to them."[27] Given the assumption that all perception is

---

*I am, to be more precise, here discussing *theistic* religious experience. For a discussion of the difference between this and nontheistic religious experience, see my *Reenchantment without Supernaturalism*, chap. 7.

sensory perception, in other words, it is difficult to explain the origin of religion, because we cannot explain it by supposing that people have actually had experiences of something holy. A more recent student of religion, Samuel Preus, likewise says that we cannot explain religious experiences by assuming that "mysterious transcendent powers beyond the realm of natural causation . . . really create this experience."[28] Therefore, says Preus, we must "explain religions— that is, their universality, variety, and persistence until now," on the assumption that "God is not given."[29] In the same vein, Robert Segal, in *Explaining and Interpreting Religion*, says that social scientists should assume that "believers never encounter God."[30]

This denial of a direct experience of God, made by modern thinkers involved in the academic study of religion, is also made by modern theologians. For example, Gordon Kaufman, who taught at Harvard Divinity School until his retirement, shares Kant's sensationist view that human perception is exclusively sensory. On this basis, Kaufman says, in response to the question of what the word "God" might refer to, "Certainly not to anything we directly experience."[31]

The Existence of God as an Actual Being

Given this impossibility of speaking either of divine activity in the world or the human experience of God, it should come as no surprise to hear that modern theologians have even rejected the existence of God as an actual being. Paul Tillich, one of the foremost theologians of the twentieth century, said that God is not *a* being but simply being itself, that which all beings have in common.[32] Accordingly, although Tillich used various terms suggesting that God is purposive, acts causally in the world, and is responsive to the world, he also pointed out that because God (in his view) is not an individual, these terms can apply to God only symbolically, not literally or even analogically.[33] Indeed, there is only one nonsymbolic statement that can be made about God, said Tillich, "namely, the statement that everything we say about God is symbolic."[34]

Other modern theologians have offered other ways of redefining the word "God" so that it no longer refers to a being to which biblical categories such as creation, providential guidance, purpose, and love can be applied. Early twentieth-century American theologian Henry Nelson Wieman, for example, defined God formally as "the source of human good." Pointing out that this definition removes the question of whether God exists, since undoubtedly there is such a thing as human good and this good must have a source, he said that the only question is what this source is. Deciding that it is creative interchange, Wieman equated God with "the process of creative interchange."[35] Swiss theologian Gerhard Ebeling, arguing that it is through language that we are created as human beings, said that the word "God" refers to the "language-situation of human beings" or, more simply, our "linguisticality."[36] German New Testament theologian Herbert Braun suggested instead that the word "God" should be taken to refer to our "co-humanity."[37] British theologian Donald Cupitt, proposing yet another definition, suggests that the word "God" refers to a cluster of ideals that we have formulated imaginatively and projected onto the universe—a repetition of the definition given decades earlier by John Dewey.[38] Gordon Kaufman also says that God is a creature of our own imaginations. Having said that the idea of God is not at all similar to the idea of a perceptual object, such as a table or a person, Kaufman says that the idea of God is "constructed imaginatively in the mind."[39] Willem Drees, believing that the one question that materialistic naturalism cannot answer is why anything exists at all, uses the word "God" to point to the transcendent ground of the world, but without any suggestion as to what this ground might be like.[40]

Modern theologians, working with these and similar definitions of God, if not dispensing with God-language altogether, have been unable to do justice to any of the eight primary doctrines of the Christian faith discussed earlier, because these primary doctrines affirm God as creating the world, acting providentially, savingly, and self-revealingly in it, as being experienced as Holy Spirit, and as being good, loving, wise, purposive, and concerned for justice.

Salvation in a Life after Death

To make a final point, modern theologians have also been unable to affirm the doctrine that God, besides working for our individual and collective salvation or wholeness in this life, also intends to bring about a more complete salvation in a life beyond bodily death. This inability is obvious in the case of materialistic naturalists such as Drees, who accepts the identist view, as shown by his statement that "in some way, I am my brain."[41] But the inability to affirm any form of salvation in a life after death has been widespread even among theologians who do not share Drees's severely limiting version of naturalism. One of these was Bultmann, who regarded the resurrection of Jesus as God's decisive act but who described the resurrection by saying that Jesus "rose into the Easter faith." To affirm that Jesus was resurrected, accordingly, seemed to say no more than that the disciples came to believe in him as God's decisive messenger.

Another example is provided by Reinhold Niebuhr, one of the most influential American theologians of the twentieth century. Although Niebuhr rejected materialism and even affirmed ongoing divine activity in the world, he did accept the modern view that the immortality of the soul is ruled out by "the unity of body and soul."[42] Niebuhr preferred the image of the resurrection of the body, but only if it was taken merely as a symbol of the "eternal significance . . . for the self as it exists in the body" and "struggles . . . in history."[43] Niebuhr, however, denied that this symbol can be given any literal meaning, because the idea that "eternity will embody, and not annul, finiteness" is, he said, "logically inconceivable."[44] This denial was especially serious in the context of Niebuhr's theology, because he undermined hope within this world, rejecting the possibility either of a coming reign of God on earth or the sanctification of individuals. He said, instead, that the "fulfillment of history lie[s] beyond history."[45] When we turn to Niebuhr's eschatology, however, we learn that the idea of a fulfillment beyond history is inconceivable.[46] If the task of the theologian is to translate the original gospel into a form that we can understand as good news today, we must conclude that Niebuhr, like the other modern theologians we have examined, failed.

We should not, however, vilify these theologians, as if they were deliberately trying to undermine Christian faith. We should not even blame them for their failures, because they were given the task of doing the impossible—to restate the Christian good news within the framework of a worldview that makes such a restatement impossible. They are no more blameworthy than the earlier theologians who, within the framework of the doctrine of *creatio ex nihilo*, could not provide a theodicy portraying the Christian God as good and loving. Like these earlier theologians, our modern theologians cannot be blamed for failing to do the impossible.

We might say, of course, that they are blameworthy for simply accepting the modern worldview, instead of revising it to make it compatible with Christian faith and more adequate in itself. Breaking free of the widely held assumptions of one's time, however, is not easy. It is even more difficult to provide an extensive critique of the worldview that dominates one's age, especially if it is thought to be sanctioned by science. Still more difficult is the task of coming up with a new worldview that is in principle capable of replacing the old one. This threefold task is one that can be performed only by a few rare individuals in which the appropriate type of intellectual preparation is combined with genius.

3. The Rise of a New Worldview

Luckily, four geniuses appeared at the beginning of the twentieth century—Henri Bergson in France, Albert Einstein in Germany, and William James and Charles Sanders Peirce in America—who were able to provide telling critiques of the late modern worldview and to suggest certain aspects of a new one.* More luckily yet, another well-prepared genius showed up in the next generation who was able to synthesize the work of these other thinkers into an inclusive worldview, one that is far more adequate for science than the late modern worldview and that provides the basis for reconciling scientific naturalism with Christian faith. I refer to Alfred North Whitehead, whom I have already occasionally quoted. Whitehead's understanding of mathematical physics was such that he was able to write an alternative formulation of Einstein's theory of general relativity, or gravity. Whitehead's concern with the relation between science and religion

---

*I have elsewhere defended the use of the term "postmodern" to describe this new worldview; see my "Reconstructive Theology" and my introduction to Griffin et al., *Founders of Constructive Postmodern Philosophy*. But I will not seek here to explain how this term, generally used with very different connotations, is appropriate.

was such that he wrote that philosophy "attains its chief importance by fusing the two, namely, religion and science, into one rational scheme of thought."[47] I will now explain how Whitehead, drawing especially on some ideas suggested by William James, achieved such a fusion, thereby bringing about the eighth major synthesis between Christian faith and scientific naturalism.

Whitehead's achievement involved the replacement of naturalism$_{sam}$ with a doctrine that can be called naturalism$_{ppp}$, meaning a prehensive-panexperientialist-panentheist version of naturalism. Naturalism$_{sam}$'s sensationist doctrine of perception is replaced by a prehensive doctrine of perception, according to which sense perception is a secondary mode of perception, derivative from a nonsensory mode of perception called "prehension." Atheism is replaced by panentheism, according to which the world exists within God. And materialism is replaced by panexperientialism, according to which the world is made up of experiencing, partially self-created events. I will now discuss each of these three doctrines, beginning with Whitehead's prehensive doctrine of perception.

4. Prehension and Nonsensory Perception

In developing this doctrine, Whitehead drew upon William James's epistemology. James, calling his position "radical empiricism," thereby implied that the sensationist empiricism inherited from the eighteenth century was superficial. Whereas Hume, focusing on clear and distinct sensory perception, claimed that we had no direct experience of causal connections, James pointed out that our experience involves a depth dimension, which does contain the experience of causal connections. This depth dimension, which is rooted in nonsensory perception, also includes moral and religious experience. It also sometimes includes telepathic feelings (James was one of the leading advocates of psychical research, and his own explorations led him to have no doubt about the reality of telepathy).[48] This "thicker and more radical empiricism," James believed, was of utmost importance to the future of religion, as he indicated in one of his famous statements: "Let empiricism once become associated with religion, as hitherto, through some strange misunderstanding, it has been associated with irreligion, and I believe that a new era of religion as well as of philosophy will be ready to begin."[49] Of course, as James knew, empiricism had been associated with irreligion not merely because of some "strange misunderstanding" but because empiricism had been equated with a superficial, sensationist empiricism, which did not allow for genuine religious or moral experience. James's *radical* empiricism allowed him to take religious experience seriously, as demonstrated by his classic, *The Varieties of Religious Experience.*

Whitehead developed James's radical empiricism more fully, showing that it provides a better basis for science than does the sensationist empiricism of naturalism$_{sam}$. This more radical empiricism, by seeing sensory perception as derivative from a nonsensory mode of prehending our environment, allows philosophers of science to explain how we can apprehend mathematical and logical forms. Also, to emphasize the fact that this nonsensory mode of perception explains our experience of causation, Whitehead calls it "perception in the mode of causal efficacy." By showing that we have a direct perception of the world beyond our minds as causally efficacious for our experience, it explains why we are not afflicted by solipsism. And by showing that this mode of perception includes that type of perception we call "memory," this doctrine shows how we know the reality of the past and thereby time. This doctrine of perception thereby provides scientists with an explanation for four of their basic concepts: the actual world, causation, the past, and time.*

Besides being far more adequate for the purposes of science, this view of perception also explains how religious experience, along with moral and aesthetic experience, can be genuine. This prehensive doctrine of perception is crucial, accordingly, for Whitehead's development of a form of naturalism that is adequate for both the scientific and the religious communities.

---

*The importance of this point can be seen by remembering that it was precisely the inability of sensory perception to provide an empirical basis for such concepts that was the stimulus for Kant's form of idealism, which then led to Hegel and then Marx. The same problem provides the basis for Alvin Plantinga's claim that he is justified in taking his Calvinistic idea of God (modified to allow for free will) as a "basic belief," meaning one that requires no support, as I discuss in the final chapter of my *Reenchantment without Supernaturalism.*

5. Panexperientialism and the Mind-Body Relation

Equally crucial, and closely related, is Whitehead's replacement of naturalism$_{sam}$'s materialism with panexperientialism. Thanks to this doctrine, Whitehead's version of naturalism is able to affirm the distinction between the mind and brain and thereby human freedom, without returning to the dualistic doctrine that led to materialism. I will explain how.

The term "panexperientialism" literally means that all things have experience. But the doctrine is not meant to be taken so literally. In the first place, the things that are said to have experience are only all *actual* things, not also ideal things, such as numbers. In the second place, experience is attributed only to true individuals, not to aggregational societies of individuals, such as sticks and stones. Examples of true individuals would be human beings, other animals, living cells, organelles, macromolecules (such as DNA), ordinary molecules, atoms, and subatomic particles such as electrons and protons. A third qualification is that to say that all things have experience does not mean that all things have *conscious* experience. Consciousness is a very high-level form of experience, enjoyed (on this planet) only by humans and other animals.

Even with these qualifications, of course, most people upon hearing of panexperientialism assume it to be self-evidently absurd. That it is *not* really self-evidently absurd, however, is suggested by the fact that it has been affirmed not only by several leading philosophers, including William James, Charles Peirce, and Henri Bergson, as well as Whitehead and the other major process philosopher, Charles Hartshorne, but also by several leading physicists. For example, evolutionary biologist C. H. Waddington endorsed Whitehead's view that all things are composed of "occasions of experience," and physicists David Bohm and B. J. Hiley say that their view implies that "in some sense a rudimentary mind-like quality is present even at the level of particle physics."[50] What reasons have these thinkers had for affirming panexperientialism?

One reason is that it allows us to solve the mind-body problem. The problem with Descartes' dualism, as we saw, was that it is impossible to understand how the mind, as a consciously experiencing entity, could interact with the brain, understood to be composed of nonexperiencing bits of matter. Materialism tried to avoid this problem by denying that the mind, with its conscious experience, is an entity distinct from the brain that "interacts" with it, saying instead that conscious experience is simply one of the brain's properties. But this did not really avoid the problem. As Colin McGinn says, materialists still have an insoluble problem, namely, "How could the aggregation of millions of individually insentient neurons generate subjective awareness?"[51]

Panexperientialism, however, rejects the premise of McGinn's argument by saying that the neurons in our brain are *not* insentient, nonexperiencing things. We can understand that the mind and brain cells can interact because, rather than being completely different in kind, they are different only in degree, with both having feelings. As Hartshorne says, "cells can influence our human experiences because they have feelings that we can feel. To deal with the influences of human experiences upon cells, one turns this around. *We* have feelings that *cells* can feel."[52]

In solving the mind-body problem, I should emphasize, panexperientialism also avoids one of the central problems in neo-Darwinian evolutionary theory, which is how experience could have first emerged. Insofar as evolutionary thinkers have presupposed either a dualist or a materialist view, this question has proved unanswerable within a naturalistic framework. For example, dualist Geoffrey Madell says that "the appearance of consciousness in the course of evolution must appear for the dualist to be an utterly inexplicable emergence . . . , which must appear quite bizarre."[53] The problem is that the emergence of experience out of nonexperiencing things would seem to be impossible. As the great evolutionist Sewall Wright once put it, "Emergence of mind from no mind at all is sheer magic."* Such magic would seem to require supernatural assistance. Indeed,

*Wright, "Panpsychism and Science," 82. Wright made this comment at a conference at which I was present. After he made it, Theodosius Dobzhansky, another great evolutionist, said, "Then I believe in magic!" Dobzhansky's comment, uttered with good humor in his deep Russian accent, brought the house down. After the laughter, however, Wright's point remained, and Dobzhansky admitted that he had no explanation of *how* experience emerged out of nonexperiencing entities, only his faith that it *did*.

one philosopher of religion, Richard Swinburne, has used this problem as evidence for the truth of supernaturalism. Saying that "God, being omnipotent, would have the power to produce a soul," Swinburne holds that "the ability of God's actions to explain the otherwise mysterious mind-body connection is [a] reason for postulating his existence."[54] Colin McGinn admits that the problem is so serious that this solution is tempting. Having said that "we have no idea" how "sentience springs from pulpy matter," he adds,

> One is tempted, however reluctantly, to turn to divine assistance.
> . . . It would take a supernatural magician to extract consciousness from matter, even living matter. Consciousness appears to introduce a sharp break in the natural order—a point at which scientific naturalism runs out of steam.[55]

As a naturalist, of course, McGinn cannot accept this solution,* which leads him to conclude that the mind-body problem will remain a permanent mystery.[56] One of the main reasons to affirm panexperientialism, therefore, is that it alone can solve, without appealing to supernatural assistance, the problem of how the mind and brain are related.

But there are also other reasons. One of these is that our most immediate relation to what we normally call the "physical world" is our relation to our own bodies. We experience them *not* as devoid of feelings but as the source of pains and pleasures. The natural interpretation of this experience is that we are feeling the feelings of our bodily cells sympathetically.

This idea, that the cells of our body have their own experiences, is now supported by scientific evidence. Experiments have shown that bacteria make decisions on the basis of memory.[57] Bacteria, being prokaryotic cells, are much more primitive than eukaryotic cells, of which our bodies are made, having emerged much earlier in the course of evolution. If bacteria have memory and make decisions, we should surely attribute experience and spontaneity to the much more complex cells composing our bodies. Furthermore, no matter how far

---

*"It is," says McGinn, "a condition of adequacy upon any account of the mind-body relation that it avoid assuming theism" (*The Problem of Consciousness*, 17 n), by which he means *supernaturalistic* theism, as his reference to a "supernatural magician" shows.

down we go in the line of true individuals, we find evidence of spontaneity, which is the best indicator of experience. For example, macromolecules, such as RNA and DNA, have been shown to manifest the properties of organisms.[58] With regard to ordinary molecules, Robert Millikan, who knew so much about them that he was called "Mr. Molecule," said that if we could see them, as we see dogs and cats, we would immediately attribute self-determination to them.[59] Finally, going all the way to the quantum level, the principle of indeterminacy in quantum physics is suggestive of the idea that an element of self-determination extends all the way down.

For these and still other reasons,[60] Whiteheadian process theologians affirm panexperientialism, and this affirmation provides many benefits. One of these benefits is that it allows us to reaffirm the reality of freedom. Dualists had been able to affirm human freedom, because, distinguishing between the mind and the brain, they could regard the mind as an individual with the power of self-determination. But dualism, while *affirming* interaction between the mind and brain, could not *explain* it, so it collapsed into materialism. As a result, the freedom that we all presuppose in practice became conceptually unintelligible. Just as a billiard ball, which is composed of billions of molecules, cannot be thought to have the power of self-determination, the brain, being composed of billions of cells, cannot be understood to be an individual with the power of self-determination. Materialists, therefore, generally consider our feeling of freedom to be an illusion.[61]

Panexperientialism, like dualism, affirms that the mind and the brain are distinct entities, which interact. Unlike dualism, however, panexperientialism can explain this interaction, because it is a *non-dualistic* interaction. That is, although the mind and the brain are numerically distinct, they are not different in kind, so their interaction is intelligible. In this way, panexperientialism can affirm the mind to be distinct from the brain. And it can hold that human beings, by virtue of their minds, are true individuals, which as such can exercise self-determination.

Another benefit is that this doctrine reopens, within a naturalistic framework, the question of life after bodily death. Recognizing this fact, Whitehead said that the question should be settled on the basis of empirical evidence, if any reliable evidence is available.[62]

Although Whitehead himself did not comment on the reliability of the evidence available in his day, I have recently examined various kinds of evidence—most of which has emerged since Whitehead wrote—and concluded that it is persuasive.[63] For Christians, therefore, the evidence provided by Jesus' resurrection can be supplemented by more recent evidence, some of which has been rigorously investigated and documented by parapsychologists and physicians.* I will explain more fully how process theology deals with the resurrection of Jesus in the final chapter.

For now I want to emphasize the fact that, although the evidence for life after death is strong, a change from naturalism$_{sam}$ to the kind of naturalism suggested by Whitehead is important if the belief in life after death is again to become a respectable belief in intellectual circles. The empirical evidence can be convincing only if people will study it, and thus far most intellectuals have been unwilling to do so. Because they believe that the mind is identical with the brain, or at least entirely dependent upon it, they believe that life after death is impossible, so that the amount and the quality of the alleged evidence for it is irrelevant.† Also, they cannot even take this alleged evidence as genuine, because most of it involves nonsensory perception—as in the perception of apparitions—which they assume to be impossible. But insofar as people see the superiority of Whitehead's form of naturalism, with its nondualistic interactionism and its prehensive doctrine of perception, these a priori objections are overcome, so that the evidence can be taken seriously.

6. Panentheism

Having explained the prehensive and panexperientialist dimensions of Whitehead's naturalism$_{ppp}$, I turn to its third dimension, panentheism.

*Several physicians have been involved in the study of near-death out-of-body experiences, which are discussed in my *Parapsychology, Philosophy, and Spirituality*, chap. 8.

†For example, materialist philosopher Kai Nielsen says that if "we think that the concept of disembodied existence makes no sense . . . then we will interpret the data differently. . . . [W]e will say, and reasonably so, even if we do not have a good alternative explanation for it, that [disembodied existence] cannot be the correct description of what went on" ("God and the Soul," 61).

I will begin with Whitehead's revision of the doctrine of creation out of nothing.

Creation out of Relative Nothingness

Most of the problems of Christian theology, I have emphasized, have been due to, or at least aggravated by, the doctrine of *creatio ex nihilo*, which was introduced at the end of the second Christian century. Whitehead returned to the biblical-Platonic view, according to which God created our world by bringing order out of chaos. His doctrine, however, still allows the language of "creation out of nothing" to be used, as long as one makes clear that the "nothing" is a relative, not an absolute, nothingness.

To explain: Our world, rather than being created out of an absolute absence of finite entities, was created out of a chaotic situation in which there were no "things" as we ordinarily understand the term. That is, when we speak of "things," we normally have in mind entities such as sticks and stones and, at a lower level, entities such as molecules, atoms, and electrons. What all these things have in common is that they endure through time. We are aware, to be sure, that an electron may not endure in quite the same sense as a rock, in that the electron can be understood to consist of a sequence of events that happen in different locations without traveling through the intervening space. We can, nevertheless, speak of the electron as enduring through time, so that it is still the "same electron" from minute to minute. However, in the chaos prior to the creation of our world, by hypothesis, there were no enduring things, but simply very brief events, happening at random. The creation of our world, in the first stages, involved the formation of very elementary enduring things, perhaps quarks, out of this chaos of events.

Whitehead derived this idea partly from relativity and quantum physics, both of which implied that the ultimate units of the world are not enduring particles but momentary events.[64] He also knew that Buddhism was based on the idea that all enduring things, including minds or souls, are analyzable into momentary events. With regard to the soul in particular, Whitehead quoted William James's observation that our "acquaintance with reality grows literally by buds or drops of perception," which come "totally or not at all."[65] The idea that the ultimate units of the actual world, the fully *actual* entities, are momentary events is further supported by the fact that some of the entities that physicists call "elementary particles" endure for less than a billionth of a second. It would surely make sense to call such entities events rather than particles.

Whitehead's technical term for these momentary events is "actual occasions." The term "occasions" emphasizes that they are events— momentary happenings—while the term "actual" emphasizes that they are the entities that are real in the fullest sense of the term. The term "actual" also emphasizes that these are the things that *act*—that exert agency. The kinds of agency they exert represents another way in which Whitehead rejects the mechanistic-materialistic view of nature, which has been common to early and late modern thought. According to that mechanistic-materialistic view, as we have seen, the ultimate units of the world, being enduring bits of matter, could exert only efficient causation—that is, causation on other things. Final causation, and hence any purposive activity, was ruled out. Whitehead's actual occasions, however, exert final as well as efficient causation. Each event arises from the totality of causal influences on it from the past. But it then completes itself by deciding exactly how to respond to those influences in light of its own aims.

The idea that actual occasions make decisions reflects the fact, discussed earlier, that all individuals have experience. To emphasize this point, Whitehead refers to actual occasions as "occasions of experience." Because all actual entities are actual *occasions* and all actual occasions are occasions of *experience*, a moment of your own experience can serve as an illustration of an actual entity. In a given moment, your experience arises out of countless influences on you: influences arising from bodily urges, such as thirst or hunger pangs; influences coming to you from beyond your body through your eyes, ears, and sense of touch; influences from memories of past events, plans, and promises; and influences from values and habits that have been developed. But even this totality of influences does not dictate how your present experience responds to those various influences. Rather, you give greater or lesser attention to the various influences, perhaps deciding to take action in relation to some of them, in light of your present purpose. Your present experience, and thereby the effect it has on the future, is finally an act of self-determination, of self-creation. In returning final or purposive causation to nature, Whitehead has thereby incorporated an element of the richer naturalism embodied in Plato, Aristotle, and magical naturalism.

Part and parcel of Whitehead's richer naturalism is his conception of the basic "stuff" of which all things are composed, which Aristotle had called the "material cause" of all things. This question was at the center of the speculations of the early Greek naturalists, with some suggesting that the basic stuff underlying all things is one of the common elements of our world, such as water, air, or earth. However, Aristotle, saying that every such thing is a combination of matter and some particular form, said that the underlying material cause of all things is *prime* matter, which is never found by itself but always as informed in some particular way. This prime matter, according to Aristotle, is purely passive. Embodiments of it, therefore, are not self-moving things, but can be moved only by something external to them. This is why Aristotle's system required an unmoved mover, a divine being that, while being unmoving, served as the ultimate source of motion for all other things.

In endorsing dualism, early modern thought denied that there is only one universal stuff embodied in all things and affirmed instead that there are two fundamental kinds of stuff. Whereas nature embodies passive, insentient matter, said Descartes, human minds are constituted by a completely different kind of stuff, namely, consciousness. Given Descartes' view of the stuff composing the body, this dualism was required in order to account for our experience and freedom. As we saw earlier, however, the problem of understanding how such radically different things could interact led late modern thinkers to reject this dualism. They thereby attempted to understand all things, including human beings, as composed only of insentient, inert matter, an attempt that resulted in the inadequacies of materialism discussed earlier.

Whitehead returned to Aristotle's view, according to which there is one underlying stuff embodied in all actual things. For Whitehead, however, that stuff is not passive but active. It is, indeed, activity itself. Whitehead called it "creativity." A move in this direction had already been made by modern physics, with its discovery not only that various kinds of energy are convertible into each other but also that energy and mass are convertible into each other—a discovery symbolized in Einstein's formula $E = mc^2$. Modern physicists, accordingly, typically think of energy as the "stuff" of all things, while emphasizing that it is a dynamic, not a passive, stuff. Whitehead accepted this development but added that "the physicists' energy is obviously an abstraction," because physics "ignores what anything is in itself." That is, in studying something, physics ignores its *intrinsic* reality, dealing only with its *extrinsic* reality, meaning the way it affects other things.[66] In order to have a concept that points to what things are in themselves as well as how they influence other things, Whitehead enlarged the notion of "energy" to "creativity." Because each unit is an occasion of experience, we could also, with Hartshorne, say that the stuff of which all things are composed is "creative experience."[67]

In any case, the main point of this enlargement for our present purposes is that creativity, or creative experience, involves two kinds of causation: An actual occasion, having received efficient causation from prior actual occasions, exerts self-causation in deciding exactly what it is going to be, with part of this decision involving its anticipation of influencing future occasions. For example, when you ask me a question, I decide how I want to respond; this is my final causation. I then shape my speech organs in order to utter the desired words. This efficient causation of my mind on my body is an example of the second kind of causation exercised by every actual occasion. In saying that creativity is the universal stuff embodied in all actual things, Whitehead was suggesting that all actual occasions—from those constituting human minds to those constituting subatomic particles—exercise final as well as efficient causation.

In saying that our world was created out of a chaos of events, Whitehead meant that it was created out of actual occasions, all of which embodied creativity and thereby an element of self-determination or freedom. His position is thereby similar to that of the Russian Orthodox theologian Nicolas Berdyaev, who said that our world was created out of *relative* nothingness. In explaining his meaning, Berdyaev distinguished between the Greek term *ouk on*, which he translated "absolute nothingness," and *me on*, which he translated "relative nothingness." Berdyaev understood this relative nothingness to be primordial freedom. Berdyaev would say, therefore, that our world was created out of "meontic freedom."[68] Whitehead, in saying that God created our world out of events embodying primordial creativity, was saying essentially the same thing.

The crucial point here is that this creativity is primordial, not created. Many theologians who affirmed creation out of absolute nothingness, as we have seen, were willing to say that God had created our world out of matter. But, they insisted, this matter had itself been created by God out of absolute nothingness, which meant that it was completely under God's control. By contrast, Whitehead rejected the view that "the ultimate creativity of the universe is to be ascribed to God's volition."[69] Just as Berdyaev referred to the primordial freedom from which our world was created as "uncreated freedom," Whitehead regarded creativity as uncreated. Of course, traditional theologians also did, in one sense. That is, creative power was uncreated in the sense that it belonged to the essence of God. But insofar as traditional theists attribute creative power to the world, they regard it as a purely voluntary gift on God's part. Whitehead, by contrast, held that creativity is primordially embodied in both God and finite actual occasions. God is unique, to be sure, in being "the aboriginal instance of this creativity."[70] As such, God is the only individual who exists necessarily. But God always exists in relation to a world, to some multiplicity of finite actual occasions—whether these actual occasions are ordered into a cosmos, such as ours, or exist merely in a state of chaos. There was never a time when God existed all alone, embodying all the creativity and hence all the power.

This world, more precisely, exists in God. This doctrine is known as panentheism, which means that all finite things are in God, an idea suggested by the statement in the book of Acts that we "live, move, and have our being" in God.* This is not pantheism, which says that all things *are* God. According to panentheism, both God and the world have their own creative power. They remain distinct, so the world's

---

*The growing popularity of this view is shown by the recent publication of a book entitled *In Whom We Live and Move and Have Our Being: Reflections on Panentheism for a Scientific Age*, edited by Philip Clayton and Arthur Peacocke.

evil does not impugn the divine goodness. But the existence of the world—some world or other—is entailed by the divine existence.

Panentheism and the Problem of Evil

This way of understanding the relation of God to the world, which involves a return to the kind of view held by Hermogenes, obviously has implications for the problem of evil, as Whitehead was fully aware. He said that traditional theism, by regarding God as having created our world out of absolute nothingness, left "no alternative except to discern in [God] the origin of all evil as well as of all good."[71] Whitehead, by contrast, thought of the creation of our world as "not the beginning of [finite] matter of fact, but the incoming of a certain type of social order."[72] That is, in creating our world, God evoked a contingent form of order out of a situation that already embodied certain principles of order—principles that are not contingent but necessary, lying in the very nature of things. We have looked at the most basic of these principles: that in addition to God there is always a multiplicity of finite actual occasions embodying creativity, with creativity involving the twofold power of self-determination and efficient causation on future events. Another necessary principle is that this twofold power of the finite actual occasions cannot be overridden by divine power. The "cannot" here is not merely a *moral* "cannot"—as it is with those traditional free will theists who say that God has made an irrevocable decision never to violate human freedom—but a *metaphysical* "cannot."

The idea that there are certain things that God cannot do is, of course, not a new idea. Traditional theists, as we have seen, said that God cannot do that which is logically self-contradictory, such as making a round square. Free will theists added the point that God cannot wholly determine the actions of creatures with freedom because *that* would be self-contradictory. Whitehead simply added the further point that, because *all* individuals necessarily have at least an iota of freedom and this freedom is inherent in the nature of the world, God cannot fully determine the activities of *any* creatures.

The idea that there are certain things that are impossible for God can also be approached in terms of the divine nature. Theologians have always said that God cannot act contrary to God's own nature. Being omniscient, God could not become ignorant of something; being omnipresent, God could not withdraw from part of the universe; being perfectly wise, God could not act foolishly. Given the agreement that God could not act contrary to the divine nature, the question of what God can and cannot do depends on how we understand the divine nature.

According to traditional theism, with its doctrine of *creatio ex nihilo*, it did not belong to the divine nature to be related to a realm of finite existents. Therefore, once God created a world, everything about the way the world was related to God was determined by the divine will. This belief was the basis for extreme voluntarism. According to Whitehead's theism, by contrast, it does belong to the divine nature to be related to a realm of finite beings—and finite beings, furthermore, that have creative power that cannot be divinely overridden. Drawing out the implications of this position, Whitehead said that "the relationships of God to the World . . . lie beyond the accidents of will," being instead "founded upon the necessities of the nature of God and the nature of the World."[73] It belongs to the very nature of God, therefore, to be related to a world of finite beings whose behavior cannot be coerced, in the sense of unilaterally determined, but can only be persuaded.

In reconceiving divine power as persuasive power, Whitehead was consciously reaffirming Plato's position. Although Plato wavered on this point, his final position was that, in Whitehead's words, "the divine element in the world is to be conceived as a persuasive agency and not as a coercive agency." In coming to this view, Whitehead added, Plato made "one of the greatest intellectual discoveries in the history of religion."[74] In endorsing this view, however, Whitehead did not see himself as endorsing a Greek as opposed to a Christian view. Rather, saying that "[t]he essence of Christianity is the appeal to the life of Christ as a revelation of the nature of God and of his agency in the world," Whitehead pointed to the elements in the New Testament account of that life that "have evoked a response from all that is best in human nature." Including in these elements "[t]he Mother, the Child, and the bare manger: the lowly man, homeless and self-forgetful, with his message of peace, love, and sympathy: the suffering, the agony, the tender words as life ebbed," Whitehead said that "the power of Christianity lies in its revelation in act, of that which Plato divined in theory."[75] Christian theologians, to be sure, soon subverted this revelation, Whitehead added, turning the Christian God into "the supreme agency of compulsion," an idea that was simply a metaphysical sublimation of the barbaric idea of the gods as "the final coercive forces wielding the thunder."[76] Whitehead, nevertheless, regarded the idea that the divine element in the world is a persuasive agency and not a coercive one as belonging to the very essence of Christianity. And in adopting this idea, Whitehead thereby overcame the main source of the problem of evil, namely, the idea that the existence of any genuine evil in our world disproves either the existence or the perfect goodness of God.

There is, however, another dimension of the problem. Although people may grant that the existence of *some* evil was inevitable, they may wonder why the world has *so much* evil, especially so many *horrendous* evils.[77] It is the enormity of evil that leads many people to doubt that our world was created by a loving deity. The idea that our world was created out of relative nothingness, rather than absolute nothingness, is also relevant to this dimension of the problem. As we have seen, this way of understanding the relation between God and the world implies that there are some principles of order inherent in the very nature of things, which are not due to a divine decision. We have already discussed some of these principles: that a world of finite events necessarily exists, that these events have at least some iota of power to determine themselves and influence future events, and that divine power cannot override this twofold power of finite events. Yet another principle is that the possibilities for good cannot be increased without also increasing the possibilities for evil.

One reason for this principle is that experiencing the higher forms of value requires great sensitivity, and this sensitivity can lead to great suffering. For example, part of our enjoyment of life comes from our sensitivity to our bodies, as in our enjoyment of exercise, good food, and sexual activity. But this same sensitivity makes us susceptible to great suffering when our bodies are injured or afflicted with disease. This sensitivity to bodily suffering we share with other animals. But human life is also susceptible to forms of suffering unknown to our dogs and cats. These distinctively human forms of suffering, such as despair produced by the thought that our lives are meaningless, are the reverse side of the distinctively human forms of value-experience, such as our capacity to enjoy literature, music, mathematics, philosophy, mystical experience, and deep friendships. Our peculiar sensitivity to ideas and values, which allows us to enjoy these distinctively human values, also opens us to the distinctively human forms of suffering, some of which are so severe as to lead to suicide.*

Another reason why increasing the possibilities for good necessarily increases the possibilities for evil is that the capacity for enjoying higher values necessarily involves greater power, and this power can be used for good or for ill. Through our greater power, we human beings can bring about forms of good beyond the capacity of any other species—forms such as medicine, educational institutions, labor-saving tools, great literature, and Beethoven piano concertos. But we are also uniquely capable of causing unparalleled forms of suffering and destruction. Only our species engages in genocide. Only our species now threatens to destroy all the higher forms of life on our planet, which it has taken God billions of years to create.

This uniquely human capacity for evil has led many antitheistic philosophers to ask their theistic friends, "Why didn't God create rational saints?" by which they mean beings who are like us in most respects, having the capacity for rationality and thereby for enjoying all the distinctively human values, but guaranteed not to sin. The Whiteheadian answer to this question is obvious: God could not have created such beings, because God could guarantee that creatures otherwise like us would not sin only by creating them devoid of freedom, and that was impossible. "Okay," the critic of theism might say, "but surely God could have made creatures who, while capable of music, mathematics, and mysticism, would have been far less dangerous." The process theist, however, denies even this claim. That claim does apply to traditional theism. According to the doctrine of creation out of absolute nothingness, none of the correlations between

*Charles Hartshorne, making the point of this paragraph, said that "chances of evil overlap with chances of good. A dead man has no chance of suffering, also none of enjoyment. The principle is universal and a priori. Tone down sensitiveness and spontaneity, and one reduces the risk of suffering but also the opportunities for depth of enjoyment" (*Reality as Social Process*, 107).

value and power that we find in our world exist necessarily. According to process theism, however, the correlations present in our world do reflect necessary truths. To bring about creatures who can enjoy the values we do was necessarily to bring about creatures as dangerous as we are. God could have avoided the possibility of all the distinctively human forms of evil only by calling off the evolutionary advance prior to the emergence of human beings. God would have had to rest content with creatures at the level of dolphins and chimpanzees.

Given this perspective, we can criticize God for the world's evil only if we can honestly say that human evil is so bad that the world would have been better off without human beings. In contrast with Stendhal's charge that "God's only excuse is that He doesn't exist," process theists say that God's excuse for the horrendous evils caused and suffered by human beings is that the possibility of such evils could have been prevented only in a world devoid of human-like beings. If one says that the complaint about evil refers not simply to human evil but all the evils suffered by living things, process theology gives the same answer: God could have precluded the possibility of all this suffering only by having not stimulated the world to bring forth life. A world devoid of life is the price for a world devoid of the possibility of suffering. Even God cannot have the good without the risk of the evil.

The Existence of God

By rejecting supernaturalism, process theology overcomes the major reasons why modern thinkers have rejected belief in a Divine Actuality: the assumption that belief in such an actuality is contrary to scientific naturalism, that it is vetoed by the world's evils, and that it is supportive of the status quo. But besides overcoming these reasons for rejecting belief in God, Whitehead's worldview also provides many positive reasons for reaffirming the reality of God. Some of these reasons involve dimensions of distinctively human experience that can best be explained in terms of the assumption, which process panentheism supports, that we are directly experiencing God all the time. This is most obviously true of the religious dimension of experience. But it is also true of our awareness of mathematical principles and normative ideals, such as logical, moral, and aesthetic norms. Unless we accept the existence of an all-inclusive actuality in which these ideal entities can exist and be given agency, the fact that human beings have always and everywhere presupposed the reality of such principles is hard to explain.

In addition to these dimensions of distinctively human experience, there are many other features of the world that are best explained by reference to the kind of divine actuality affirmed by process theists. I refer to the order of the world, the repeated occurrence of novelty in the evolutionary process, the upward trend of this process, and the beauty of the world.

Although I cannot develop these arguments here, I have elsewhere shown that process theology contains at least thirteen distinct arguments, which together constitute a very strong cumulative case, for the truth of panentheism.[78] Many of these arguments are, to be sure, similar to arguments that had been developed by traditional theists, such as Thomas Aquinas. However, insofar as these arguments were taken to be evidence for the existence of the God of traditional theism, they were undermined by the problem of evil and the other reasons for doubting the existence of God. The reasons for believing in God were balanced out by the reasons for not believing in God. Once we see, however, that these traditional arguments are better understood as arguments for the God of naturalistic panentheism, we can see that there are many reasons for accepting the reality of God and none for rejecting it. Thanks to naturalistic theism, arguments for the reality of God can again be persuasive.

Variable Divine Causation

The recovery of persuasive arguments for God is an important event for Christian faith, of course, only if the Divine Reality referred to is adequate for supporting the primary doctrines of this faith. As we saw earlier, the "God" spoken of by many modern philosophers and theologians is not, because this "God" is not an actual being, or at least not one that can act variably in the world so that some events can be especially revelatory of God. Many conservative to fundamentalist theologians assume that, just for this reason, Christian faith requires belief in a supernatural deity—one who can exert variable causation by occasionally interrupting the world's normal causal patterns. A distinctive feature of Whiteheadian process theism is that, while being a form of naturalistic theism, it affirms variable divine causation in the world.

Whitehead, in articulating this idea, was developing a position suggested by William James. In addition to the physical world, which we know through sensory perception, James held that there is "an altogether other dimension of existence" from which "our ideal impulses originate." Against the view that "the world of the ideal has no efficient causality, and never bursts into the world of phenomena at particular points," James said that he found "no intellectual difficulty in mixing the ideal and the real worlds together by interpolating influences from the ideal region among the forces that causally determine the real world's details."[79] More precisely, against those who say that the Divine Reality relates only to the world as a whole, so that the ideal world "cannot get down upon the flat level of experience and interpolate itself piecemeal between distinct portions of nature," James affirmed that God *can* so act.[80] In other words, James affirmed particular providence, the idea that God's prevenient grace is different for different events, depending upon the situation. This affirmation of particular providence, however, did not imply supernaturalism, because God always acts in the same way *formally*—by providing what James called "ideal impulses" to "personal centres of energy." While being formally the same, however, this divine influence could be variable in content, insofar as different ideals are relevant to different situations.*

---

*James, *The Varieties of Religious Experience*, 510, 507. Unfortunately, James, taking "naturalism" to mean that the world knowable through the senses is all there is, referred to his own position as "piecemeal supernaturalism" (403–05). Although James thereby meant only to indicate that God is distinct from the world and presents different ideals for different events, his use of the term "supernaturalism" could easily be interpreted to mean that this variable divine influence involved supernatural interruptions of the world's basic causal processes. James was, in fact, thus misinterpreted by John Mackie (*Miracle of Theism*, 12, 13, 182). Such misinterpretations illustrate why it is better to use the contrast between "supernaturalism" and "naturalism" strictly for the contrast between views that do and do not allow for interruptions of the world's basic causal principles. In terms of that contrast, James, like Whitehead after him, was a theistic naturalist.

Whitehead developed this doctrine, explicitly affirming "particular providence for particular occasions."[81] Like James, Whitehead affirmed that God acts in the world by providing ideals, which he called "initial aims."[82] He said, accordingly, "There are experiences of ideals—of ideals entertained, of ideals aimed at, of ideals achieved, of ideals defaced. This is the experience of the deity of the universe."[83] In providing these aims, God seeks to persuade each occasion of experience to actualize the best possibility open to it, given its concrete situation.[84] In the final chapter, I will explain how this doctrine allows us to affirm a robust version of Christian faith while also affirming religious pluralism.

NOTES

1. Wright, *God Who Acts*, 120.
2. Gilkey, "Cosmology, Ontology, and the Travail of Biblical Language," 29, 31.
3. Ibid., 32, 35, 37.
4. Bultmann, *Kerygma and Myth*, 19, 37–38.
5. Bultmann, *Jesus Christ and Mythology*, 15.
6. Ibid., 65.
7. Ibid., 62, 68; Bultmann, *Kerygma and Myth*, 196.
8. Bultmann, *Jesus Christ and Mythology*, 61–62.
9. Gilson, "The Corporeal World and the Efficacy of Second Causes," 222.
10. Gilkey, "Cosmology, Ontology, and the Travail of Biblical Language," 36–37.
11. Drees, *Religion, Science and Naturalism*, 18.
12. Bultmann, *Jesus Christ and Mythology*, 15.
13. Drees, *Religion, Science and Naturalism*, 12.
14. Hick, *The Metaphor of God Incarnate*, 12.
15. Ibid., 7.
16. Ibid., 99, 104, 106.
17. Hick, *God and the Universe of Faiths*, 94.
18. Ibid., 51.
19. Wiles, *The Remaking of Christian Doctrine*, 93.
20. Ibid., 102.
21. Wiles, "Religious Authority and Divine Action," 186.
22. Wiles, *The Remaking of Christian Doctrine*, 38.
23. Wiles, "Religious Authority and Divine Action," 182.
24. Ibid., 188.
25. Kant, *Religion within the Limits of Reason Alone*, 163.
26. Smart, "Religion and Science," 222–23.

27. Durkheim, *Elementary Forms of the Religious Life*, 57.

28. Preus, *Explaining Religion*, 174.

29. Ibid., xv.

30. Segal, *Explaining and Interpreting Religion*, 71.

31. Kaufman, *In Face of Mystery*, 415.

32. Tillich, *Systematic Theology*, 1:214.

33. Ibid., 1:238, 271–73, 280.

34. Ibid., 2:9–10.

35. See Wieman, *The Source of Human Good*.

36. Ebeling, *God and Word*, 27–29.

37. Braun, "The Problem of New Testament Theology," 183.

38. See Cupitt, *Taking Leave of God*; and Dewey, *A Common Faith*.

39. Kaufman, *In Face of Mystery*, 323.

40. Drees, *Religion, Science and Naturalism*, 237, 266–68.

41. Ibid., 184.

42. Niebuhr, *The Nature and Destiny of Man*, 2:298.

43. Ibid., 2:311–12.

44. Ibid., 2:297.

45. Niebuhr, *Beyond Tragedy*, ix.

46. Niebuhr, *The Nature and Destiny of Man*, 2:297–98.

47. Whitehead, *Process and Reality*, 15.

48. See my *Parapsychology, Philosophy, and Spirituality*, 46–48.

49. James, *Essays in Radical Empiricism*, 270.

50. Waddington, *The Evolution of an Evolutionist*, 4–5; Bohm and Hiley, *The Undivided Universe*, 386. Another great scientist who affirmed panexperientialism, Sewall Wright, is mentioned below in the text. For the philosophers mentioned, see Griffin et al., *Founders of Constructive Postmodern Philosophy: Peirce, James, Bergson, Whitehead, and Hartshorne*.

51. McGinn, *The Problem of Consciousness*, 1.

52. Hartshorne, *The Logic of Perfection and Other Essays in Neoclassical Metaphysics*, 229.

53. Madell, *Mind and Materialism*, 140–41.

54. Swinburne, *The Evolution of the Soul*, 198–99.

55. McGinn, *The Problem of Consciousness*, 45.

56. Ibid., 213.

57. See Adler and Tse, "Decision-Making in Bacteria," and Goldbeter and Koshland, "Simple Molecular Model for Sensing Adaptation."

58. See Keller, *A Feeling for the Organism*.

59. Charles Hartshorne once reported in a lecture that Millikan made this comment in his presence.

60. For a more complete discussion, see chap. 7 of my *Unsnarling the World-Knot*.

61. For examples, see my *Unsnarling the World-Knot*, 37–40, 163–217.

62. Whitehead, *Religion in the Making*, 111.

63. See my *Parapsychology, Philosophy, and Spirituality*, esp. chaps. 4–8.

64. Whitehead, *Science and the Modern World*, 34–35.

65. Whitehead, *Process and Reality*, 68, quoting James, *Some Problems of Philosophy,* chap. 10.

66. Whitehead, *Science and the Modern World*, 36, 153.

67. Hahn, ed., *The Philosophy of Charles Hartshorne*, 690, 720.

68. Berdyaev, *The Destiny of Man*, 22–35; Berdyaev, *Truth and Revelation*, 124.

69. Whitehead, *Process and Reality*, 225.

70. Ibid.

71. Whitehead, *Science and the Modern World*, 179.

72. Whitehead, *Process and Reality*, 96.

73. Whitehead, *Adventures of Ideas*, 168.

74. Ibid., 166.

75. Ibid., 167.

76. Ibid., 166.

77. See Adams, *Horrendous Evils and the Goodness of God*.

78. See my *Reenchantment without Supernaturalism*, chap. 5.

79. James, *The Varieties of Religious Experience*, 510.

80. Ibid., 511–12.

81. Whitehead, *Process and Reality*, 351.

82. Ibid., 244.

83. Whitehead, *Modes of Thought*, 103.

84. Whitehead, *Process and Reality*, 84, 244.

Chapter 4

Christian Faith

From Arrogance to Timidity to
Respectful Confidence

*I*n the first chapter, I argued that scientific naturalism, as it has developed over the past two centuries, has been a very ambiguous movement. On the one hand, it has involved the recovery and entrenchment of a great truth, namely, that there are no supernatural interruptions of the world's most fundamental causal processes. On the other hand, it has distorted this truth by embodying it in a sensationist, atheistic, materialistic version that rules out the possible truth of our deepest moral and religious convictions and is even woefully inadequate for science itself.

In the second chapter, I argued that Christianity has also been a very ambiguous movement. On the one hand, the primary doctrines of Christian faith constitute a great truth that has universal importance. On the other hand, Christianity as it developed historically distorted this great truth by allowing it to be overshadowed by secondary and tertiary doctrines that distracted attention from the primary doctrines and even contradicted them. Central to this distortion, I suggested, was the idea of divine omnipotence, especially as supported by the doctrine that our world was created out of absolute nothingness, which implies that God has absolute power over every detail in it. This doctrine led to many distortions of the Christian faith. For one thing, by producing an insoluble problem of evil, it undermined the primary doctrine that our world has been created by a Divine Being who is good and loving. The idea of divine omnipotence also lent support to the social, economic, and political status quo, thereby undermining other primary doctrines of Christian faith, namely, those saying that God is concerned about justice and seeks the "reign of God on earth," for which we ask in the Lord's Prayer. A third distortion was the shift of attention away from the divine love to Christianity itself as the "one true religion" in such a way as to undermine the doctrine of the divine love. Having briefly mentioned this third distortion in the first and second chapters, I will in this final chapter focus on it and its overcoming.

As the title of this chapter suggests, Christian faith in its traditional form was terribly arrogant. For example, in spite of clear statements in the New Testament that God desires all people to be saved, the church in the third century developed the dictum that "outside the church, there is no salvation." In the fifteenth century, the Council of Florence declared that "those not living within the Catholic Church . . . cannot become participants in eternal life, but will depart 'into the eternal fire prepared for the devil and his angels,' unless before the end of life [they] have been added to the flock."[1]

This exclusivist doctrine of salvation was closely related to the supernaturalist Christology that was developed in the early centuries, which became official through the Councils of Nicaea and Chalcedon in the fourth and fifth centuries, respectively. This Christology, in spite of its nuances, essentially said, in the words of John Cobb, that Jesus was "the transcendent, omnipotent, omniscient ruler of the world . . . walking about on earth in human form."[2] As John Hick points out, these councils, in saying that Jesus was the second person of the Holy Trinity incarnate, implied "that Christianity, alone among the religions, was founded by God in person," so that it was "God's own religion in a sense in which no other can be."[3]

This arrogant attitude lay behind the Christian persecution of Jews, which forms one of the sorriest chapters in Christian history and led to the Nazi-induced Holocaust in the twentieth century. This attitude also lay behind the crusades against the Islamic world, the aftereffects of which are still very much alive today. This attitude also lay behind the American theology of "manifest destiny,"[4] which justified what David Stannard calls the "American Holocaust,"[5] meaning the virtual extermination of the Native Americans.

However, while these effects of traditional Christian theology were working themselves out in the eighteenth, nineteenth, and twentieth centuries, the status of Christianity in the nature of things was being radically rethought by Christian theology, at least by the type of Christian theology that remained in touch with cultural developments—that is, the modern liberal theology that I discussed in the third chapter. This radical thinking had both negative and positive implications.

The negative implications were due primarily to the fact that scientific naturalism, which was emerging and becoming culturally dominant, was understood as naturalism$_{sam}$. As a result, modern liberal theology lost confidence and became extremely timid. For example, when John Tyndall in the latter part of the nineteenth century declared, on behalf of those advocating the materialistic version of scientific naturalism, "We claim, and we shall wrest from theology, the entire domain of cosmological theory,"[6] modern liberal theologians let them do it. It is now widely assumed in intellectual circles that theologians have nothing to contribute to the discussion of cosmology, the nature of our universe.

One of the positive results of the influence of scientific naturalism—and here it was simply naturalism$_{ns}$ that was important—was the emergence of religious pluralism. As Christian thinkers rejected the idea that God's activity in founding Christianity was different in kind from God's activity in other religious traditions, they realized that the relation of Christianity to these other religions could not be settled a priori but needed to be based on an actual examination of the fruits of the respective religions—the kinds of people they produce. On this basis, many theologians concluded that Christianity is not the only means through which God brings religious truth and salvation to humankind.

Another factor that led these theologians to a pluralistic form of Christian faith is that they came to see the exclusive view of Christianity—according to which it is the one true religion, through which salvation is exclusively mediated—to be in severe tension with the primary Christian doctrine of God's universal love. Arnold Toynbee argued, for example, that "the Jewish and Christian vision of God as being love" makes it seem "unlikely that He would not have made other revelations to other people as well."[7] Likewise, John Hick, who as a young man held a very conservative version of Christian faith, reports that later, in wrestling with the problem of evil, he came to wonder how "to reconcile the notion of there being one, and only one, true religion with a belief in God's universal saving activity."* Hick came to see that the idea that "only by responding in faith to God in Christ can we be saved" would imply that "infinite love has ordained that human beings can be saved only in a way that in fact excludes the large majority of them."[8] This kind of thinking has led many Christian theologians to affirm religious pluralism, which is, in the words of Roman Catholic theologian Paul Knitter, the acceptance of the "possibility that other religions may be ways of salvation just as much as is Christianity."[9]

However, although the humility and respect involved in this pluralistic attitude is an extremely positive development, the dominant direction taken by pluralism has been a mixed blessing. As Alan Race points out, most versions of pluralism have tended to lead to a "debilitating relativism"—the view that all religions are equally true in a way that makes them equally false.[10] As a result, the timidity of modern liberal theology has been increased by the hitherto dominant version of religious pluralism.

The question before us now, I suggest, is whether we can, without returning to supernaturalistic interpretations of Christian faith, with their arrogance, move beyond this timidity to respectful confidence. That is, can we recover confidence in the universal truth and importance of the primary doctrines of Christian faith while, at the same time, accepting the great truth of scientific naturalism and manifesting respect for the other great religious traditions? In other words, can we develop a theology that, while being both naturalistic and pluralistic, is robustly Christian?

I provided the background for my positive answer to this question in the previous chapter, in which I explained the version of naturalism developed by Alfred North Whitehead, which has become the basis for the movement known as process theology. By replacing materialistic naturalism with panentheistic naturalism, it provides a basis for again understanding the world as God's creation, and yet not in such a way as to reopen the problem of evil. Panentheism does not

*Hick, *God Has Many Names*, 17. For perhaps the best treatment of the way in which Christian exclusivism aggravates traditional theism's already difficult problem of evil, see Ogden, *Is There Only One True Religion or Are There Many?* 33–41.

reopen this problem because it is a naturalistic theism, according to which divine interruptions of the world's causal processes are not possible. Nevertheless, this form of theism affirms variable divine causation in the world, so it is possible, as Isaiah 43:19 declares, for God to "do a new thing." This point is crucial for the development of a form of Christian faith that can, while rejecting supernaturalism, be robust. I will illustrate this point by suggesting how we can reconceive the doctrine of God as Trinitarian.

Reconceiving God as Trinitarian

As developed within traditional Christian theology, the doctrine of the Trinity was part and parcel of its supernaturalism. The idea that God is a trinity of three persons was used, for one thing, to support the doctrine of creation out of absolute nothingness. One problem produced by that doctrine of creation was that it seemed to contradict the New Testament assertion that "God is love," that it belongs to the very nature of God to be loving. Love is a relationship between two or more beings. If there were only one being, it could not be loving. But the doctrine of creation out of absolute nothingness seemed to imply just this, that prior to the creation of the world, God existed all alone. A solution to this problem was suggested by those theologians who thought of God as a social trinity—a society of three persons. The biblical statement that God is love was said to refer primarily to the love that the members of the Trinity have for each other. God did not need the world in order to be loving by nature. This position is still held by many supernaturalists. For example, Austin Farrer, a prominent Anglican theologian in the twentieth century, argued that God does not need a world, being "what he is above and apart from the world," because there is a "life of God in God, above and before all worlds," this being the "fellowship of Blessed Trinity."[11] The doctrine of the Trinity has thereby served as a tertiary doctrine to support the secondary doctrine of *creatio ex nihilo*.

   This idea of a trinity of three persons was also used to support the supernaturalistic Christology discussed earlier in relation to the Christian claim to be the one true religion. As John Hick says, the idea that Christianity alone was founded by God in person was based on the doctrine that Jesus "was God—more precisely, God the Son, the second person of the Holy Trinity—incarnate."[12] According to this view, God was present to the prophets merely as Holy Spirit. In Jesus alone was God the Son incarnate.

The Trinitarian doctrine of God has also been central to traditional theology's epistemic supernaturalism, to the idea that certain doctrines have come to us through supernatural revelation. Thomas Aquinas, for example, used the Trinity as a clear example of the difference between "natural" and "revealed" theology. Through natural theology—that is, through unaided human reasoning—said Thomas, we can know that God exists. But it is only through supernatural revelation that we learn that God is a divine trinity of persons. This doctrine was said to be supernatural also in the sense that, even after it is revealed, we cannot understand it. That is, God is revealed to be three persons and yet one being—a completely unified being. How this can be was said to be a mystery, beyond our grasp, and the history of attempts to make sense of this doctrine have certainly confirmed this view.

Given this intimate connection between Trinitarianism and supernaturalism, the idea of employing the idea of God as threefold to develop a naturalistic Christian theology might seem unpromising. However, another twentieth-century Anglican theologian, Charles Raven, brought out its potential. Understanding the divine threefoldness to mean that God is Creator, Redeemer, and Sanctifier, pointed out Raven, involves a repudiation of Marcion's dualism, according to which our world was created by an evil deity, different from the redeeming God manifest in Jesus. By including the book of Genesis in the Christian canon, the early church repudiated this dualism, declaring creation and redemption to be two actions of one and the same divine reality. Unfortunately, Raven said, traditional theology missed the full significance of this identification, taking it to mean that the one God operates in two different ways, using coercive power to create the world, then using persuasive love to save human beings. But, argued Raven, the true significance of the rejection of Marcionism is that we should understand God's *creative* activity in the light of the nature of God's *saving* activity as manifested in Jesus.[13]

Christians, therefore, should reject the idea of a "dual mode of divine operation" and should believe "in love not force as the ultimate power."[14]

The Nicene Creed was, of course, explicitly directed not against Marcion but against Arius, who said that the preexistent Logos that was incarnate in Jesus was not really divine but a subordinate being, the first of the creatures. Nicaea, with its affirmation that God the Father and the Divine Logos are *homoousion*—of the same substance or essence—declared that that which was incarnate in Jesus was the Divine Actuality itself. Theologians at the time, accepting the idea that God is both omnipotent and impassible (incapable of suffering), took this affirmation to mean that the divine element in Jesus was likewise omnipotent and impassible. This doctrine, enunciated in 325, then led to the long struggle to understand how this divine nature of Jesus was related to his human nature, which was *not* omnipotent or impassible. The Council of Chalcedon in 451 declared that Jesus was both truly divine and truly human while being one undivided person. How this could be was recognized to be a mystery, like the doctrine of the Trinity, which could only be adored, not understood.

Raven, however, suggested a different understanding of the significance of the Nicene Creed—as embodied in the creed of the Council of Constantinople, which in 381 declared the Holy Spirit to be equally divine. We should, Raven said, understand this creed in terms of its implications for the divine *modus operandi*—the divine mode of action. To say that *God* was truly present and active in Jesus should be taken to mean that Jesus, who did not manifest impassible omnipotence, reveals to us the divine mode of activity. One implication of this point is that God's final victory over evil will not be achieved through coercive omnipotence.[15] Whitehead had made a similar point in saying that "[t]he essence of Christianity is the appeal to the life of Christ as a revelation of the nature of God and of his agency in the world."[16]

Interpreted in this way, the doctrine of the Trinity can serve as a shorthand summary of naturalistic theism, with its rejection of the idea that God, having two modes of divine acting, can occasionally interrupt the world's normal causal processes. Given Raven's interpretation, the doctrine of the Trinity means that creation, saving revelation, and sanctification are brought about by one and the same God, operating in one and the same way—the way of love, which is the way of persuasion, not coercive force. Thus understood, the doctrine of the Trinity says that God acts in relation to all events persuasively, never interrupting this normal method by occasionally acting coercively to bring about effects unilaterally. Raven emphasizes, in particular, that God works in this way in creating, in becoming incarnate, and in sanctification. I will now indicate how we can understand these three processes as occurring through divine persuasion.

Creation through Persuasion

Traditional Christian thinkers, taking the book of Genesis to be a historical account of the origin of our world and the first humans, believed that our world, in its present form, was created virtually all at once, about four thousand years before Christ. Given that belief, it was natural for these thinkers to assume that the world was created through omnipotent coercion. It would have been virtually impossible for them to have imagined Raven's interpretation, according to which the world was created through the kind of power manifest in Jesus, the power of persuasion through attraction. Even if they could have been convinced that the world's basic elements are the kinds of things that could respond to attractive possibilities, they would have pointed out that the method of persuasion would have taken a very long time—perhaps billions of years.

One of the great discoveries of modern science, of course, is that our world has indeed been about fifteen billion years in the making. Insofar as earlier Christians believed that the world was literally created in six days, the time available for God to create the world has been multiplied almost a trillion times. And this seems to be one of those cases in which the *quantitative* difference is so great that it implies a *qualitative* difference. That is, whereas a timeline of six days implied that the world was created through coercive intelligence, a timeline of approximately fifteen billion years implies that the world's creation, if guided by intelligence, must have been guided by intelligence that acts persuasively, not coercively. Otherwise why would the task have taken so long? The doctrine that our world was brought about by divine persuasion is, therefore, compatible with its age.

Beyond merely being compatible with the evidence that our world has come about through a long, slow, evolutionary process, however, the doctrine of creation through divine persuasion allows us to provide a far better interpretation of this process than that provided by the currently dominant theory, neo-Darwinism. That theory, an explicitly antitheistic one, seeks to show how the world, with its apparent design, could have come about blindly, without intelligent guidance of any sort. As Richard Dawkins says in *The Blind Watchmaker*, the purpose of the theory is to answer the question of how living things, which seem "too beautifully 'designed' to have come into existence by chance," nevertheless did so. Darwin's answer, explains Dawkins, was "by gradual, step-by-step transformations from simple beginnings." The key point, emphasizes Dawkins, is that "[e]ach successive change in the gradual evolutionary process was simple enough, *relative to its predecessor,* to have come into existence by chance."[17]

However, a severe problem with this theory, which has challenged it from the outset, is that the fossil record does not support this picture of gradual evolution through tiny steps. Although Darwin was committed to the dictum that "nature makes no jumps," the fossil record suggests that evolution has proceeded by means of a series of jumps from one species to another. If evolution had proceeded in the way that Darwinism requires, the fossil record should contain tens of thousands of transitional forms, but it in fact contains virtually no such forms. Once a new species emerges, it tends to stand still, undergoing no significant change for millions of years.[18] It seems, accordingly, that there would not have been time for the evolution of the present forms of life, most of which have developed since the beginning of the Cambrian explosion only about 540 million years ago. Most of the basic designs of multicellular life, furthermore, were formed during this "explosion," within a span of only five million to ten million years.[19]

Closely related to this *empirical* problem faced by neo-Darwinism is the *conceptual* problem of understanding how new species could come about through purely chance mutations. The problem is that each living species is "irreducibly complex," which means that it is a functioning unit, in which the functioning of each part implies the functioning of the other parts. Therefore, for a change to result in a new viable species (upon which natural selection could then operate), a number of major changes would have to occur *simultaneously*. In the evolution from amphibia to reptiles, for example, the new kind of egg would have required at least eight simultaneous innovations.[20] Can we really suppose that such coordinated changes have, time and time again, occurred purely by chance? Darwin himself had pointed out the problem: "If it could be demonstrated that any complex organ existed which could not possibly have been formed by numerous, successive, slight modifications, my theory would absolutely break down."[21] It would seem that it breaks down at almost any point one looks.

The neo-Darwinian tradition is committed to this extreme gradualism because of its atheism and nominalism. By its "nominalism," I mean its denial that there are any Platonic forms in the nature of things. Neo-Darwinists deny the existence of such forms because, like other atheists, they deny the existence of an all-inclusive Divine Actuality, in which such forms could exist and be rendered efficacious for the world. Just as other atheists must deny the existence of mathematical, moral, and aesthetic forms, neo-Darwinists deny the existence of organic forms. If such forms did exist, we would not need to say that the evolutionary jumps were purely chance affairs. We could suppose that the various preexisting forms have served as "attractors," giving organisms a coherent possibility to aim at. Because of its commitment to atheism and thereby nominalism, however, neo-Darwinism must say that all changes are tiny ones that occur purely by chance. The neo-Darwinian account of how our world came about seems to be refuted, therefore, by the twofold problem that evolution apparently neither occurred, nor could have occurred, in the way the theory requires.

Whitehead's form of naturalism can solve both of these problems. One of the main reasons Whitehead came to affirm the existence of God, after having long been an agnostic or even an atheist, was to explain how forms of various types can exist and be efficacious in the world. This God acts in the world, as we have seen, exclusively by means of presenting forms to the creatures as attractive possibilities, to persuade them to move forward. Whitehead's position includes, furthermore, an account of how creatures can, by prehending novel forms in God, incorporate them into themselves in such a way as to pass them on to future generations.

This account of how evolution is conceivable is one of many ways in which Whitehead's theistic naturalism proves itself superior to the atheistic naturalism that is presently dominant. It provides one of the bases, therefore, for Christian thinkers to recover confidence in the illuminating power of the theistic perspective, and thereby to challenge the notion that theological ideas have no contribution to make to cosmology.

Furthermore, once the scientific community comes to understand that theism need not mean supernaturalism, it may be able to accept this contribution, thereby moving to a theistic version of naturalism. Many scientists today realize that the present form of naturalism leads to highly implausible theories. For example, Harvard's Richard Lewontin, one of our most brilliant biologists, has admitted the "patent absurdity" of some of the explanations that are required from a purely materialistic standpoint. He believes, however, that this standpoint must be maintained, in spite of the absurdities to which it leads. Why? "[W]e cannot allow a Divine Foot in the door," he says, because "[t]o appeal to an omnipotent deity is to allow that at any moment the regularities of nature may be ruptured, that miracles may happen."[22] Once scientists come to see that there is a third alternative, so that they are not forced to choose between materialism and supernaturalism, they may realize that theism, as Plato saw long ago, can undergird the scientific enterprise rather than threaten it.

Incarnation through Persuasion

The next question is whether we can understand the incarnation of God in Jesus as having occurred through persuasion rather than as requiring a supernatural exception to God's normal way of acting in the world.* This is possible if we hold that God was related to Jesus in essentially the same way as God was related to the prophets, a view held by some of the early Christians, sometimes called Ebionites. Such a Christology would be inadequate, of course, if we assumed that an essential part of the christological task of our time is to reaffirm the doctrines enunciated in the creeds of Nicaea, Constantinople, and Chalcedon. But most of those doctrines are secondary or even tertiary doctrines, which we need not try to reaffirm. What is essential is to support our primary doctrine about Jesus—that God was present in him in such a way as to reveal God's character, purpose, and mode of operation.

In process philosophy, this kind of incarnation could have resulted from Jesus' experience of—Jesus' prehensions of—God's influence on him. Causation between two individuals does not involve an external relation, like the impact of one billiard ball on another, but involves an internal relation, in which the cause enters, in a sense, into the effect. Whitehead says that his philosophy "is mainly devoted to the task of making clear the notion of 'being present in another entity.'"[23] In application to God, this point means that, because God influences all events, God is present in all events. Whitehead even says that "the world lives by its incarnation of God in itself."[24] Within this framework, then, there is no problem of understanding how God could have been incarnate in Jesus. The only question is how God could have been present in such a way as to make Jesus a decisive revelation of God.

Having previously worked out such an explanation at some length,[25] I will here simply summarize the main points. First, God always presents initial aims toward the best possibilities open to the individual, given its past history and present situation. These initial aims constitute, therefore, prevenient grace. Second, the best possibilities for different individuals can differ radically. For example, the best possibilities for a human being differ radically from the best possibilities for electrons or mice; the best possibilities for Christians in Grand Rapids differ greatly from the best possibilities open to Hindus

---

*Part of Austin Farrer's reason for insisting on supernaturalism was his belief that Christian salvation required what he called a "true incarnation," which required Jesus to have been "very God become man" ("The Prior Actuality of God," 184–85, 190).

in Bombay; the best possibilities for a person who has responded pos-
itively to the divine persuasion all his or her life will differ radically
from the best possibilities for someone who has consistently resisted
the divine persuasion. The nature of the divine aims and therefore the
prevenient grace for different individuals will, therefore, differ radically. Third, the aims for some individuals will reflect the general
divine aim more directly than the aims for other individuals. Fourth,
assuming that the history of Israel, including especially the messages
of the prophets, involved genuine revelation of the divine will, a
devout person such as Jesus, growing up in that tradition, would be
well suited to receive divine aims highly reflective of the general aim
of God for the world, especially the human world. Fifth, we can
understand Jesus as one in whom God was incarnate in such a way
that it is appropriate for us to apprehend Jesus as a decisive revelation of God's character, purpose, and mode of operation.

It may seem that for Christians to believe this—that they rightly
take Jesus as their decisive revelation of God because God was incarnate in him in a special way—is to believe that their religion is superior to all others. But this need not be the case. Although this topic is
much too complex to deal with briefly, let me indicate a direction of
thought by quoting a statement by John Cobb:

> Consider the Buddhist claim that Gautama is the Buddha. That is
> a very different statement from the assertion that God was incar-
> nate in Jesus. The Buddha is the one who is enlightened. To be
> enlightened is to realize the fundamental nature of reality, its insub-
> stantiality, its relativity, its emptiness. . . . That Jesus was the incar-
> nation of God does not deny that Gautama was the Enlightened
> One.[26]

Lying behind Cobb's statement is the idea that different religions
are not necessarily in competition with each other, because they can
be answering different questions. They can also be oriented around
different ultimates. Whereas the theistic religions, such as Judaism,
Christianity, and Islam, are oriented around God, nontheistic religions, such as many forms of Buddhism and Hinduism, are oriented
around creativity, which they may call "emptiness" or "nirguna Brah-
man." Given this kind of perspective, in which religions can be

regarded as complementary to each other, we can retain confidence in our own religion while having respect for other religions as genuine mediators of truth and saving values.[27]

Sanctification through Persuasion

I turn now to the issue of eschatology. Christian faith involves hope for the ultimate victory, in some sense, of good over evil. Is it possible to understand this victory as being brought about by divine persuasion? Most Christian theologians have assumed not. This seems, in fact, to be the main reason why many of them hang on to the traditional doctrine of omnipotence, even though it creates such a terrible problem of evil. Certainly much of the imagery involved in the biblical depictions of the last things, especially in the book of Revelation, has led many Christians to assume that the ultimate defeat of evil will require overwhelming divine force, even violence. For example, one theologian says that although Jesus may have used nonviolent persuasion during his ministry, "Jesus will at the end bring all criminals (sinners) to judgment by violent means (overthrowing the armies of the Antichrist by force and casting sinners into hell)."[28] In the same vein, a book entitled *Armageddon* says,

> In His first coming to earth, Jesus Christ was born in a stable . . .
> in a time of comparative peace. . . . The second coming of Jesus
> Christ to earth will be no quiet manger scene. It will be the most
> dramatic and shattering event in the entire history of the universe.
> . . . Cities will literally collapse, islands sink, and mountains disappear. Huge hailstones, each weighing a hundred pounds, will fall
> from heaven. . . . [T]he rulers and their armies who resist Christ's
> return will be killed in a mass carnage.[29]

In other words, no more Mister Nice Guy!

From Raven's point of view, if we rightly understand the implications of the doctrine of the Trinity, this kind of theology is heretical. Truly rejecting the Arian heresy that the preexistent one incarnate in Jesus was a subordinate deity, says Raven, means recognizing "Christ's way of redemption as universally characteristic and effective. If we agree that God uses other means . . . in respect of the Last

Judgment . . . we are Arians, however much we may recite the Nicene Creed."[30] God, in other words, will not resort to coercive power to bring about the ultimate victory of good over evil. Indeed, if we say that the power of love cannot overcome the power of evil, we are in effect denying that love is the ultimate power of the universe.

The possibility of understanding how love can overcome our subjugation to evil is connected with another primary doctrine of Christian faith, namely, the idea that although the divine purpose, as revealed in Jesus, is to bring about as much salvation, or wholeness, as possible in this world, it is also, to quote my own earlier statement, "to bring about an even more complete salvation in a life beyond bodily death."

In order to be able to conceive of this possibility, of course, we must believe that life after death is possible. Most modern liberal theology has denied this, whether explicitly or only implicitly, due to its acceptance of the late modern worldview. The general assumption, by both liberal and conservative theologians, is that life after death would require supernatural intervention. That would be the case, of course, if one were thinking in terms of a resurrection of the physical body. In fact, the realization that the resurrection of the body would require absolute omnipotence was, Gerhard May reports, one of the factors leading early Christian theologians to move toward the idea of *creatio ex nihilo*.[31]

The first Christians, however, evidently did not think in these terms. The aspostle Paul, who is the first witness we have to the resurrected Jesus, distinguished between the physical body, which dies, and the body of the resurrected life, which is a spiritual body. Furthermore, as my Claremont colleague Gregory Riley has shown in his book *Resurrection Reconsidered*, the idea that the resurrection of Jesus involved the resurrection of his physical body emerged only near the end of the century, in response to the views of some gnostics. The earliest Christians had characteristically thought in terms of the "resurrection of the soul."

This doctrine has been affirmed, in fact, by process theologian John Cobb, in an article called "The Resurrection of the Soul." As Cobb points out, this formulation affirms the main point of each of the two standard formulations, which have long been in competition.

That is, like the phrase "immortality of the soul," the "resurrection of the soul" suggests that life after death is rooted in a power inherent in the nature of the soul, so that no supernatural assistance is needed. However, like the phrase "resurrection of the body," the phrase "resurrection of the soul" suggests that the new life after death is due to divine grace. And this is the case. If the human soul now has the capacity to survive bodily death and hence to exist in a new environment, this capacity exists only because of repeated divine initiatives over many billions of year, which were necessary for human beings to become possible and then actually to emerge. Also, besides the fact that initial aims from God are necessary for every event, significantly new divine aims would be needed for the soul, after having hitherto lived in relation to a physical body, to make a transition to existence in a radically new environment.

In any case, we can perhaps now, through a new form of naturalism combined with the empirical evidence provided by parapsychology, think of the end of our present life not as the end of our journey with God but simply as the beginning of its next phase. If so, we can conceive that divine grace, working entirely through the attractive power of love, might sanctify us all. There would be no need for the divine violence of casting sinners into hell. God would, instead, love the hell out of us.

There is a parallel here with the possibility of thinking of creation through persuasion. This became possible only because our vision of the time available to God expanded enormously. Analogously, just as the early Christians thought of the world as having been created within a week only a few thousand years ago, they also thought that the end of the world would come soon, so that the defeat of evil, just like the creation of the world, would require coercive omnipotence. But if we think of life after death as a continuing journey, we can think of salvation as a gradual process of sanctification, in which the divine love gradually purges us of our enslavement to demonic values. A version of this idea was developed, of course, in the Catholic doctrine of purgatory, but even there the time available to divine grace was assumed to be quite short, compared with the time assumed to be necessary for salvation in Hindu and Buddhist teaching. We should remember, as Father Virgil Cordano, a beloved Catholic priest in Santa Barbara, likes to say, that God has all the time in the world. With this time, God may, as the "Battle Hymn of the Republic" puts it, "transfigure you and me."

In this final chapter, I have suggested an approach through which we can recover confidence in the primary doctrines of Christian faith, seeing them as truths important for all peoples, and even for science—and yet in such a way as not to deny the truths of the other great traditions, including the tradition of scientific naturalism.

NOTES

1. Quoted in Cobb, *Beyond Dialogue*, 9.
2. Cobb, *Christ in a Pluralistic Age*, 163.
3. Hick, *A Christian Theology of Religions*, 15.
4. See Merk, *Manifest Destiny and Mission in American History*, and Stephanson, *Manifest Destiny*.
5. See Stannard, *American Holocaust*.
6. Tyndall, *Fragments of Science*, 530.
7. Toynbee, "What Should Be the Christian Approach to the Contemporary Non-Christian Faiths?" 161.
8. Hick, *Philosophy of Religion*, 117–18.
9. Knitter, *No Other Name?* 17.
10. Race, *Christians and Religious Pluralism*, 78.
11. Farrer, "The Prior Actuality of God," 191, 180.
12. Hick, *A Christian Theology of Religions*, 15.
13. Raven, *Is War Obsolete?* 128.
14. Ibid., 182.
15. Raven, *The Theological Basis of Christian Pacifism*, 65.
16. Whitehead, *Adventures of Ideas*, 167.
17. Dawkins, *Blind Watchmaker*, 43.
18. Wesson, *Beyond Natural Selection*, 207; Stanley, *The New Evolutionary Timetable*, 90; Newell, "The Nature of the Fossil Record," 267; Denton, *Evolution;* 162–64.
19. See my discussion in *Religion and Scientific Naturalism*, 280.
20. Denton, *Evolution*, 218–19.
21. Darwin, *The Origin of Species*, 171.
22. Lewontin, "Billions and Billions of Demons," 31.
23. Whitehead, *Process and Reality*, 50.
24. Whitehead, *Religion in the Making*, 156.
25. See my *A Process Christology*.
26. Cobb, *Transforming Christianity and the World,* 140.
27. For more on this Whiteheadian complementary pluralism, see Cobb, *Beyond*

Dialogue; Cobb, *Transforming Christianity and the World*; Griffin, "The Two Ultimates and the Religions" (in Griffin, *Reenchantment without Supernaturalism*); and Griffin, ed., *Deep Religious Pluralism.*

28. Macaulay, "Review of *Nuclear Holocaust and Christian Hope*," 60.

29. Walvoord and Walvoord, *Armageddon;* quoted in Jewett, *Jesus against the Rapture*, 16.

30. Raven, *The Theological Basis of Pacifism,* 65.

31. May, *Creatio Ex Nihilo,* 129, 132, 137.

References

Adams, Marilyn McCord. *Horrendous Evils and the Goodness of God*. Ithaca, N.Y.: Cornell University Press, 1999.

Adler, Julius, and Wing-Wai Tse. "Decision-Making in Bacteria." *Science* 184 (June 21, 1974): 1292–94.

Augustine. *Augustine: Earlier Writings*. Library of Christian Classics 6. Philadelphia: Westminster Press, 1953.

Baker, Gordon, and Katherine J. Morris. *Descartes' Dualism*. London: Routledge, 1996.

Barbour, Ian. *Religion in an Age of Science*. San Francisco: Harper & Row, 1990.

———. *When Science Meets Religion: Enemies, Strangers, or Partners?* San Francisco: HarperSanFrancisco, 2000.

Barnard, L. W. *Justin Martyr: His Life and Thought*. Cambridge: Cambridge University Press, 1967.

Baumer, Franklin. *Religion and the Rise of Scepticism*. New York: Harcourt, Brace & Co., 1960.

Berdyaev, Nicolas. *The Destiny of Man*. New York: Harper & Row, 1960.

———. *Truth and Revelation*. New York: Collier Books, 1962.

Bohm, David, and B. J. Hiley. *The Undivided Universe: An Ontological Interpretation of Quantum Theory*. London: Routledge, 1993.

Boyle, Robert. *The Works of the Honourable Robert Boyle*. London: A. Millar, 1744.

Braun, Herbert. "The Problem of New Testament Theology." In *The Bultmann School of Biblical Interpretation: New Directions?* edited by Robert Funk, 169–83. New York: Harper & Row, 1965.

Brooke, John Hedley. *Science and Religion: Some Historical Perspectives*. Cambridge: Cambridge University Press, 1991.

Buckley, Michael J. *At the Origins of Modern Atheism*. New Haven, Conn.: Yale University Press, 1987.

Bultmann, Rudolf. *Jesus Christ and Mythology*. New York: Charles Scribner's Sons, 1958.

————. *Kerygma and Myth: A Theological Debate.* Edited by Hans Werner Bartsch. New York: Harper & Row, 1961.

Calvin, John. *Institutes of the Christian Religion.* Edited by John T. McNeill. Translated by Ford Lewis Battles. Library of Christian Classics 20–21. Philadelphia: Westminster Press, 1960.

Chihara, C. "A Gödelian Thesis regarding Mathematical Objects: Do They Exist? And Can We Perceive Them?" *Philosophical Review* 91 (1982): 211–17.

Clayton, Philip, and Arthur Peacocke, eds. *In Whom We Live and Move and Have Our Being: Reflections on Panentheism for a Scientific Age.* Grand Rapids: Wm. B. Eerdmans Publishing Co., 2003.

Cobb, John B., Jr. *Beyond Dialogue: Toward a Mutual Transformation of Christianity and Buddhism.* Philadelphia: Fortress Press, 1982.

————. *Christ in a Pluralistic Age.* Philadelphia: Westminster Press, 1975.

————. "The Resurrection of the Soul." *Harvard Theological Review* 80, no.2 (1987): 213–27.

————. *Transforming Christianity and the World: A Way beyond Absolutism and Relativism.* Edited by Paul F. Knitter. Maryknoll, N.Y.: Orbis Books, 1999.

Cobb, John B., Jr., and Clark H. Pinnock, eds. *Searching for an Adequate God: A Dialogue between Process and Free Will Theists.* Grand Rapids: Wm. B. Eerdmans Publishing Co., 2000.

Cottingham, John G., Robert Stoothoff, and Dugald Murdoch, eds. *The Philosophical Writings of Descartes.* Vol. 1. Cambridge: Cambridge University Press, 1985.

Crombie, A. C. "Marin Mersenne." In *Dictionary of Scientific Biography*, edited by C. G. Gillispie, 9:316–22. New York: Charles Scribner's Sons, 1974.

Cupitt, Donald. *Taking Leave of God.* New York: Crossroad, 1981.

Darwin, Charles. *The Origin of Species* (1872). New York: Mentor Books, 1958.

Darwin, Francis, ed. *The Life and Letters of Charles Darwin.* New York: D. Appleton, 1896.

Davis, Stephen T., ed. *Encountering Evil: Live Options in Theodicy.* Louisville, Ky.: Westminster John Knox Press, 2001.

Dawkins, Richard. *The Blind Watchmaker: Why the Evidence of Evolution Reveals a Universe without Design.* New York: W.W. Norton & Co., 1987.

Denton, Michael. *Evolution: A Theory in Crisis.* London: Burnett Books, 1991.

Dewey, John. *A Common Faith.* New Haven, Conn.: Yale University Press, 1934.

Drees, Willem. *Religion, Science and Naturalism.* Cambridge: Cambridge University Press, 1996.

Durkheim, Emile. *The Elementary Forms of the Religious Life.* Translated by Joseph Ward Swain. New York: Free Press, 1963 (French original, 1912).

Easlea, Brian. *Witch Hunting, Magic and the New Philosophy: An Introduction to the Debates of the Scientific Revolution, 1450–1750.* Atlantic Highlands, N.J.: Humanities Press, 1980.

Ebeling, Gerhard. *God and Word.* Philadelphia: Fortress Press, 1967.

Erickson, Millard J. *Christian Theology.* Grand Rapids: Baker Book House, 1985.

Farley, Edward, and Peter Hodgson. "Scripture and Tradition." In *Christian Theology: An Introduction to Its Traditions and Tasks*, 2d ed., edited by Peter C. Hodgson and Robert H. King, 61–87. Philadelphia: Fortress Press, 1985.

Farrer, Austin. "The Prior Actuality of God." In Farrer, *Reflective Faith: Essays in Philosophical Theology,* edited by Charles C. Conti. London: SPCK, 1972.

Field, Hartry. *Science without Numbers.* Princeton, N.J.: Princeton University Press, 1980.

Fredriksen, Paula. *From Jesus to Christ: The Origins of the New Testament Images of Jesus.* New Haven, Conn.: Yale University Press, 1988.

Gilkey, Langdon B. "Cosmology, Ontology, and the Travail of Biblical Language." In *God's Activity in the World: The Contemporary Problem*, edited by Owen Thomas, 29–43. Chico, Calif.: Scholars Press, 1983.

Gilson, Etienne. "The Corporeal World and the Efficacy of Second Causes." In *God's Activity in the World: The Contemporary Problem*, edited by Owen Thomas, 213–30. Chico, Calif.: Scholars Press, 1983.

Goldbeter, A., and Daniel E. Koshland, Jr. "Simple Molecular Model for Sensing Adaptation Based on Receptor Modification with Application to Bacterial Chemotaxis." *Journal of Molecular Biology* 161, no. 3 (1982): 395–416.

Griffin, David Ray, ed. *Deep Religious Pluralism* (forthcoming).

———. "Divine Goodness and Demonic Evil." In *Evil and the Response of World Religion*, ed. William Cenkner, 223–400. St. Paul: Paragon House, 1997.

———. *Evil Revisited: Responses and Reconsiderations.* Albany, N.Y.: State University of New York Press, 1991.

———. *God, Power, and Evil: A Process Theodicy*. Philadelphia: Westminster Press, 1976; reprinted with a new preface. Lanham, Md.: University Press of America, 1991.

———. "In Response to William Hasker." In *Searching for an Adequate God: A Dialogue between Process and Free Will Theists,* edited by John B. Cobb, Jr., and Clark H. Pinnock, 246–62. Grand Rapids: Wm. B. Eerdmans Publishing Co., 2000.

———. "Materialist and Panexperientialist Physicalism: A Critique of Jaegwon Kim's *Supervenience and Mind.*" *Process Studies* 28, nos. 1–2 (spring–summer 1999): 4–27.

———. "On Hasker's Attempt to Defend His Parity Claim." *Process Studies* 29, no. 2 (fall–winter 2000): 233–36.

———. *Parapsychology, Philosophy, and Spirituality: A Postmodern Exploration.* Albany, N.Y.: State University of New York Press, 1997.

———. "Postmodern Theology for the Church." *Lexington Theological Quarterly* 28, no. 3 (fall 1993): 201–60.

———. *A Process Christology*. Philadelphia: Westminster Press, 1973; reprinted with a new preface. Lanham, Md.: University Press of America, 1990.

———. "Process Theology and the Christian Good News: A Response to Classical Free Will Theism." In *Searching for an Adequate God: A Dialogue between*

Process and Free Will Theists, edited by John B. Cobb, Jr., and Clark H. Pinnock, 1–38. Grand Rapids: Wm. B. Eerdmans Publishing Co., 2000.

———. "Reconstructive Theology." In *The Cambridge Companion to Postmodern Theology,* edited by Kevin J. Vanhoozer, 102–08. Cambridge: Cambridge University Press, 2002.

———. *Reenchantment without Supernaturalism: A Process Philosophy of Religion.* Ithaca, N.Y.: Cornell University Press, 2001.

———. *Religion and Scientific Naturalism: Overcoming the Conflicts.* Albany, N.Y.: State University of New York Press, 2000.

———. "Traditional Free Will Theodicy and Process Theodicy: Hasker's Claim for Parity." *Process Studies* 29, no. 2 (fall–winter 2000): 209–26.

———. *Unsnarling the World-Knot: Consciousness, Freedom, and the Mind-Body Problem.* Berkeley, Calif.: University of California Press, 1998.

Griffin, David Ray, et al. *Founders of Constructive Postmodern Philosophy: Peirce, James, Bergson, Whitehead, and Hartshorne.* Albany, N.Y.: State University of New York Press, 1993.

Hahn, Lewis Edwin, ed. *The Philosophy of Charles Hartshorne.* The Library of Living Philosophers 20. La Salle, Ill.: Open Court, 1991.

Harman, Gilbert. *The Nature of Morality: An Introduction to Ethics.* New York: Oxford University Press, 1977.

Hartshorne, Charles. *The Logic of Perfection and Other Essays in Neoclassical Metaphysics.* La Salle, Ill.: Open Court, 1962.

———. *Reality as Social Process: Studies in Metaphysics and Religion.* Glencoe, Ill.: Free Press, 1953.

Hellman, G. *Mathematics without Numbers.* Oxford: Oxford University Press, 1989.

Hick, John. *A Christian Theology of Religions: The Rainbow of Faiths.* Louisville, Ky.: Westminster John Knox Press, 1995.

———. *God and the Universe of Faiths.* London: Macmillan, 1975.

———. *God Has Many Names.* Philadelphia: Westminster Press, 1982.

———. *The Metaphor of God Incarnate.* London: SCM Press, 1993.

———. *Philosophy of Religion.* 3d ed. Englewood Cliffs, N.J.: Prentice-Hall, 1983.

Hintikka, Jaakko. "Cogito, Ergo Sum: Inference or Performance." *Philosophical Review* 71 (1962): 3–32.

Hodge, Charles. *Systematic Theology* (1872). 3 vols. Grand Rapids: Wm. B. Eerdmans Publishing Co., 1989.

Hooykaas, R. *Natural Law and Divine Miracle: A Historical-Critical Study of the Principle of Uniformity in Geology, Biology, and Theology.* Leiden: E. J. Brill, 1959.

Horsley, Richard. *Jesus and Empire: The Kingdom of God and the New World Disorder.* Minneapolis: Fortress Press, 2003.

———. *Jesus and the Spiral of Violence: Popular Jewish Resistance in Roman Palestine.* San Francisco: Harper & Row, 1987.

Jacob, James. "Boyle's Atomism and the Restoration Assault on Pagan Naturalism." *Social Studies of Science* 8 (1978): 211–33.

————. *Robert Boyle and the English Revolution: A Study in Social and Intellectual Change*. New York: B. Franklin, 1978.

James, William. *Essays in Radical Empiricism* (in a volume with *A Pluralistic Universe*), edited by Ralph Barton Perry. New York: E. P. Dutton, 1971.

————. *Some Problems of Philosophy*. London: Longmans, Green & Co., 1911.

————. *The Varieties of Religious Experience* (1902). New York: Penguin Books, 1985.

Jay, Martin. "The Debate over Performative Contradiction: Habermas versus the Poststructuralists." In Jay, *Force Fields: Between Intellectual History and Cultural Critique*, 25–37. New York: Routledge, 1993.

Jewett, Robert. *Jesus against the Rapture*. Philadelphia: Westminster Press, 1979.

Johnson, Phillip E. *Reason in the Balance: The Case against Naturalism in Science, Law, and Education*. Downers Grove, Ill.: InterVarsity Press, 1993.

Kant, Immanuel. *Religion within the Limits of Reason Alone*. Translated by Theodore M. Greene and Hoyt H. Hudson. New York: Harper & Row, 1960.

Kaufman, Gordon D. *In Face of Mystery: A Constructive Theology*. Cambridge, Mass.: Harvard University Press, 1993.

Keller, Catherine. *The Face of the Deep: A Theology of Becoming*. New York: Routledge, 2003.

Keller, Evelyn Fox. *A Feeling for the Organism: The Life and Work of Barbara McClintock*. San Francisco: W. H. Freeman, 1983.

Kim, Jaegwon. *Supervenience and Mind: Selected Philosophical Essays*. Cambridge: Cambridge University Press, 1993.

Kim, Stephen S. *John Tyndall's Transcendental Materialism and the Conflict between Religion and Science in Victorian England*. Lewiston, N.Y.: Mellen University Press, 1996.

Klaaren, Eugene M. *The Religious Origins of Modern Science: Belief in Creation in Seventeenth-Century Thought*. Grand Rapids: Wm. B. Eerdmans Publishing Co., 1977.

Knitter, Paul. *No Other Name? A Critical Survey of Christian Attitudes toward the World Religions*. Maryknoll, N.Y.: Orbis Books, 1985.

Koyré, Alexandre. *From the Closed World to the Infinite Universe*. Baltimore: Johns Hopkins University Press, 1957.

Lamont, Corliss. *The Illusion of Immortality*. 4th ed. New York: Frederick Ungar, 1965.

Lenoble, Robert. *Mersenne ou la naissance du méchanisme*. Paris: Librairie Philosophique J. Vrin, 1943.

Lerner, Gerda. *The Creation of Patriarchy*. New York: Oxford University Press, 1986.

Levenson, Jon D. *Creation and the Persistence of Evil: The Jewish Drama of Divine Omnipotence*. San Francisco: Harper & Row, 1988.

Lewontin, Richard. "Billions and Billions of Demons." *New York Review of Books*, January 9, 1997, 28–32.

Lindberg, David C. *The Beginnings of Western Science: The European Scientific Tradition in Philosophical, Religious, and Institutional Context, 600 B.C. to A.D. 1450*. Chicago: University of Chicago Press, 1992.

Luther, Martin. *On the Bondage of the Will.* Translated by J. I. Packer and O. R. Johnston. Grand Rapids: Fleming H. Revell, 1957.

Macaulay, Ranald. Review of *Nuclear Holocaust and Christian Hope* by Ronald J. Sider and Richard K. Taylor. In *Who Are the Peacemakers? The Christian Case for Nuclear Deterrence,* edited by Jerram Barrs, 55–61. Westchester, Ill.: Crossway Books, 1983.

Mackie, John. *The Miracle of Theism: Arguments for and against the Existence of God.* Oxford: Clarendon Press, 1982.

Madell, Geoffrey. *Mind and Materialism.* Edinburgh: Edinburgh University Press, 1988.

May, Gerhard. *Creatio Ex Nihilo: The Doctrine of "Creation out of Nothing" in Early Christian Thought.* Translated by A. S. Worrall. Edinburgh: T. & T. Clark, 1994.

McClenon, James. *Wondrous Events: Foundations of Religious Belief.* Philadelphia: University of Pennsylvania Press, 1994.

McGinn, Colin. *The Problem of Consciousness: Essays toward a Resolution.* Oxford: Basil Blackwell, 1991.

Merk, Frederick. *Manifest Destiny and Mission in American History.* New York: Alfred A. Knopf, 1963.

Mosse, George L. "Puritan Radicalism and the Enlightenment." *Church History* 29 (1960): 424–39.

Murphy, Michael. *The Future of the Body: Explorations in the Further Evolution of Human Nature.* Los Angeles: Jeremy Tarcher, 1992.

Needham, Joseph. *Science and Civilization in China.* 7 vols. Cambridge: Cambridge University Press, 1954–1996.

Neiman, Susan. *Evil in Modern Thought: An Alternative History of Philosophy.* Princeton, N.J.: Princeton University Press, 2002.

Newell, Norman D. "The Nature of the Fossil Record." *Proceedings of the American Philosophical Society* 103, no. 2 (1959): 264–85.

Niebuhr, Reinhold. "As Deceivers Yet True." In Niebuhr *Beyond Tragedy.* New York: Charles Scribner's Sons, 1937.

———. *The Nature and Destiny of Man.* 2 vols. New York: Charles Scribner's Sons, 1943.

———. "The Truth in Myths." In *The Nature of Religious Experience,* edited by J. S. Bixler, R. L. Calhoun, and H. R. Niebuhr, 117–35. New York: Harper & Brothers, 1937.

Nielsen, Kai. "God and the Soul: A Response to Paul Badham." In *Death and Afterlife,* edited by Stephen T. Davis, 53–64. London: Macmillan, 1989.

Oates, Whitney J., ed. *Basic Writings of St. Augustine.* 2 vols. New York: Random House, 1948.

Ogden, Schubert M. *Is There Only One True Religion or Are There Many?* Dallas: SMU Press, 1992.

Pagels, Elaine. *The Gnostic Gospels.* New York: Random House, 1979.

Plantinga, Alvin. "Reply to the Basingers on Divine Omnipotence." *Process Studies* 11, no. 1 (spring 1981): 25–29.

Preus, J. Samuel. *Explaining Religion: Criticism and Theory from Bodin to Freud.* New Haven, Conn.: Yale University Press, 1987.

Putnam, Hilary. *Words and Life,* edited by James Conant. Cambridge, Mass.: Harvard University Press, 1994.

Race, Alan. *Christians and Religious Pluralism: Patterns in Christian Theology of Religions.* Maryknoll, N.Y.: Orbis Books, 1983.

Rauschenbush, Walter. *A Theology for the Social Gospel.* Nashville: Abingdon Press, 1945.

Raven, Charles. *Is War Obsolete? A Study of the Conflicting Claims of Religion and Citizenship.* London: George Allen & Unwin, 1935.

———. *The Theological Basis of Christian Pacifism.* New York: Fellowship Publications, 1951.

Riley, Gregory. *Resurrection Reconsidered: Thomas and John in Controversy.* Minneapolis: Fortress Press, 1995.

Ruether, Rosemary. *Faith and Fratricide.* New York: Seabury Press, 1974.

Sanders, E. P. *Jesus and Judaism.* Philadelphia: Fortress Press, 1985.

Schmookler, Andrew Bard. *The Parable of the Tribes: The Problem of Power in Social Evolution.* Boston: Houghton Mifflin, 1986.

Schüssler Fiorenza, Elisabeth. *In Memory of Her: A Feminist Theological Reconstruction of Christian Origins.* New York: Crossroad, 1990.

Searle, John R.. *Minds, Brains, and Science: The 1984 Reith Lectures.* London: British Broadcasting Corporation, 1984.

Segal, Robert J. *Explaining and Interpreting Religion: Essays on the Issue.* New York: Peter Lang, 1992.

Smart, J. J. C. "Religion and Science." In *Philosophy of Religion: A Global Approach,* edited by Stephen H. Phillips, 217–24. Fort Worth: Harcourt Brace, 1996.

Stanley, Steven M. *The New Evolutionary Timetable.* New York: Basic Books, 1981.

Stannard, David E. *American Holocaust: The Conquest of the New World.* New York: Oxford University Press, 1992.

Stephanson, Anders. *Manifest Destiny: American Expansion and the Empire of Right.* New York: Hill & Wang, 1995.

Suchocki, Marjorie. *The Fall to Violence: Original Sin in Relational Theology.* New York: Continuum, 1994.

Swinburne, Richard. *The Evolution of the Soul.* Oxford: Clarendon Press, 1986.

Thomas Aquinas. *Summa Contra Gentiles.* Translated by Vernon J. Bourke. Notre Dame, Ind.: University of Notre Dame Press, 1997.

———. *Summa Theologica.* Translated by Fathers of the English Dominican Province. Revised by Daniel J. Sullivan. Chicago: Encyclopaedia Britannica, 1952.

Thomas, Owen C., ed. *God's Activity in the World: The Contemporary Problem.* AAR Studies in Religion 31. Chico, Calif.: Scholars Press, 1983.

Tillich, Paul. *Systematic Theology.* 2 vols. Chicago: University of Chicago Press, 1951, 1957.

Toynbee, Arnold. "What Should Be the Christian Approach to the Contemporary Non-Christian Faiths?" In *Attitudes toward Other Religions: Some Christian Interpretations*, edited by Owen C. Thomas, 153–71. New York: Harper & Row, 1969.

Tyndall, John. *Fragments of Science*. 5th ed. London: Longmans, Green & Co., 1876.

Vartanian, Aram. *Diderot and Descartes: A Study of Scientific Naturalism in the Enlightenment*. Princeton, N.J.: Princeton University Press, 1953.

Waddington, C. H. *The Evolution of an Evolutionist*. Edinburgh: Edinburgh University Press, 1975.

Walvoord, John F., and John E. Walvoord. *Armageddon: Oil and the Middle East Crisis*. Grand Rapids: Zondervan Publishing House, 1976.

Waszink, J. H. *Tertullian: The Treatise against Hermogenes*. London: Westminster, 1956.

Wesson, Robert G. *Beyond Natural Selection*. Cambridge, Mass.: MIT Press, 1991.

Whitehead, Alfred North. *Adventures of Ideas* (1933). New York: Free Press, 1967.

———. *Modes of Thought* (1938). New York: Free Press, 1968.

———. *Process and Reality* (1929). Corrected edition, edited by David Ray Griffin and Donald W. Sherburne. New York: Free Press, 1978.

———. *Religion in the Making* (1926). New York: Fordham University Press, 1996.

———. *Science and the Modern World* (1925). New York: Free Press, 1967.

Wieman, Henry Nelson. *The Source of Human Good*. Chicago: University of Chicago Press, 1946.

Wiles, Maurice. "Religious Authority and Divine Action." In *God's Activity in the World: The Contemporary Problem*, edited by Owen Thomas, 181–94. Chico, Calif.: Scholars Press, 1983.

———. *The Remaking of Christian Doctrine*. London: SCM Press, 1974.

Williamson, Clark M. *Has God Rejected His People? Anti-Judaism in the Christian Church*. Nashville: Abingdon Press, 1982.

Wright, G. Ernest. *God Who Acts: Biblical Theology as Recital*. London: SCM Press, 1952.

Wright, Sewall. "Panpsychism and Science." In *Mind in Nature: Essays on the Interface of Science and Philosophy*, edited by John B. Cobb, Jr., and David Ray Griffin, 79–88. Washington, D.C.: University Press of America, 1977.

Index

*NOTE: The numbers in **bold** after some terms with multiple citations indicate pages on which the terms are defined.*